A Journey in Faith

Richard P. Belcher

ISBN 1-883265-27-4

Richbarry Press

105 River Wood Drive, Fort Mill, SC 29715

Printed in the United States of America

An Introduction to the Journey Series

This is the thirteenth book in a continuing series about Ira F. Pointer and his struggles to understand and preach the truth of the Word of God. For the reader's help, a very brief summary of each book is given in this introduction to the series.

Book One, *A Journey in Grace*, finds Ira in the fall of 1970 studying for the ministry in Collegetown. His pursuit in this book becomes Calvinism---what is it and does the Bible teach it?

Book Two, *A Journey in Purity*, begins in the winter of 1971, as Ira faces the problem of impurity in the lives of his church members.

Book Three, *A Journey in Authority*, is set in the year of 1972, a few months after book two. Ira is in a new church, Unity Baptist Church. The theological search this time concerns church government---elder leadership versus congregational rule.

Book Four, *A Journey in the Spirit*, has its setting in the Spring of 1973. Ira meets Durwood Girvin, the new pastor at First Baptist Church. The doctrinal pursuit is the Holy Spirit, as he finds himself in conflict with Girvin on the subject.

Book Five, *A Journey in Inspiration*, finds its setting in the summer of 1976, as Ira heads to seminary, and finds himself unintentionally caught up in the inerrancy battle.

Book Six, *A Journey in Providence*, takes place in 1981. Ira is taking a rest, having finished the Master of Divinity degree, before further study. The book begins with the kidnapping of Dink's son, which results in Ira and Dink studying the providence of God in the book of Job, as they seek the lost son.

Book Seven, *A Journey in Eschatology*, originates during the summer of 1982. Ira faces a double challenge---to find his birth parents and to write a book on the subject of eschatology. Both pursuits prove to be much more difficult than he had anticipated.

Book Eight, *A Journey in Salvation*, commences during the fall of 1983. Ira now has joined the faculty of a seminary, where he is teaching, while he pursues doctoral studies. The doctrinal search is in the area of salvation, as Ira and Dink seek to help a fallen pastor understand the basics of true salvation.

Book Nine is titled *A Journey in Revival---True or False*? The setting is the Spring of 1985. Ira has completed his doctoral work and is still teaching at the seminary. The theological conflict concerns an end-time revival in their city.

Book Ten is titled *A Journey in Baptism*, and unfolds in the fall of 1985. Ira and one of his students discuss objectively the doctrine of baptism, with Ira setting forth a covenantal Baptist view, and the student the Paedobaptist understanding of baptism. At the same time Ira is pulled into a puzzling sniper mystery.

Book Eleven, titled *A Journey in Roman Catholicism*, takes place in the fall of 1986. Ira is accused of having written a book declaring that he is going to become a Roman Catholic, and the evidence is so persuasive that he is relieved of his duties as a professor at the Baptist Seminary. Dink disappears, as they seek to uncover this web of deceit which has engulfed them.

Book Twelve, titled *A Journey in God's Glory*, takes place in the early part of 1988. Ira encounters a pastor, who ministered for his own glory for years. But then he hits the wall, when his wife leaves him and disappears to get away from her overbearing and self-centered husband. He seeks Ira's help concerning a life and ministry for the glory of God.

Book Thirteen, *A Journey in Faith,* is set in the summer of 1989. Ira and Dink are pulled into the mystery of the elimination of all the records of a pastor and his books, even though he had spent forty-three years pastoring in a small mountain town. Many lessons on faith are learned by Ira and Dink, as they seek to find the answers to this mystery.

Though each book is part of a continuing series, a person can read any book separately with understanding, as each plot stands as a single unit, and each theological study is independent as well. However, some characters from the previous books appear in later books as part of the plot, which a reading of the books in order will help the reader understand the characters better in the process.

1 Is God Omnipotent?

It is easy to assert the omnipotence of God! God is all-powerful! God is all-powerful over all things! God is all-powerful over all things in all places of existence! God is all-powerful over all things in all places of existence at all times! Thus we are saying that His power is infinite, unchangeable, uncontrolled by man, and unbounded in its nature! He alone controls and channels His power for His purposes and His will. Thus true Christians would agree with these statements and confirm these ideas with great joy and strong emphasis!

But when it comes to the reality of our daily lives, I wonder how many believers would quickly bail out, when confronted by difficulties and setbacks in their individual experience. God is omnipotent but…! If He is omnipotent, then why the setbacks for Christians? Why the difficulties, as we seek to do His will? Why such delays, as we wait for His will to come to pass? Why His silence so often for such long periods, as we long for Him to show His power in our behalf? Why doesn't He do something in these moments of agony and uncertainty? Anything! Now!

How many believers surrender to false ideas in such moments as these? This cannot be God's will for my life, we conclude, for there are too many roadblocks! Or on the other hand, we reason that something must be God's will for our lives, just because God does not stop us in any way ---no roadblocks! In simple words, do we not sometimes conclude that God's sovereign omnipotence is clear to us in the easy times of life, but not so certain in the difficult moments of our existence, as we are quick to ask in those hours, "Where is God?" or "Why did God allow this?"

I wonder, when I hear people say things like this, if such people have ever read the Bible. Maybe we all need to be reminded to read His Word more---and apply it to our lives! What about Abraham, as he waited for the promised seed until he was a hundred years old? What about Joseph, as he waited for years to escape prison---not once but twice? What about Moses, as he sought to do God's will in helping the Children of Israel in Egypt? And on and on we could go, drawing attention to such situations in the Bible, regarding the servants of God and their hours of waiting on Him.

Is it not true, contrary to our fleshly thinking, that God often, as we wait on Him to work His will, makes our way seem impossible, whereby there is no way we can explain the why of it, let alone see a way of escape from it? And why would He do this? Is it not so that when the longed for answer or solution to our dilemma comes, no one will doubt that He, the omnipotent God, was the agent of our deliverance? He makes it undeniably clear that it was not our power or any other human force or being which was the power behind the solution to our impossible situation. Only God!

These thoughts just recently have not only been pressed upon my mind anew, but undeniably confirmed in my life with great force! God has demonstrated these truths afresh in another of our "journeys." He has shown me the power and the reality and the practicality of the doctrine of His omnipotence, and the necessity of faith in His power, for the living of the Christian life and my daily ministry.

It all began with a simple and normal conversation with a student concerning his doctoral dissertation---but it didn't end there!

2 Two Men Named William Sangster?

It is not often that a doctoral student asks to write his dissertation on a subject from the life of a theologian who is unfamiliar to me. But, then, that was not the only unique thing about this student's request. He had been assigned to me by the doctoral committee to oversee his writing, but I had received nothing from him about a possible subject.

He introduced himself to me as William Sangster, and I sized him up as a very serious young man, some where in his late twenties. I say he was serious, because there seemed to be something troubling him about the subject of his dissertation.

"Dr. Pointer, I don't know if you will let me write on this theologian or not, but I want you to know that this is more than just a dissertation for me. It is a life search and quest for me, and it may be a very difficult thing for me to do. Nonetheless, I want to pursue a certain man and the whole of his theology or one area at least!"

"Well, suppose you tell me who the man is, and why this is more than just a dissertation for you, and I will be glad to seek to honor your desire, if at all possible!" I replied.

"The man's name is William Sangster!" he said, expecting some shock from me, I am sure, as I did note that he bore the same name. "As I said, this is more than just a dissertation for me," he continued, "because I think he is my great-great-grandfather or something like that to me! The only problem is that, though he wrote a number of books, many of them commentaries, and though he pastored the same church for forty-three years, there is no strong and firm record of his books or of his pastorate!"

"No records?" I asked with some skepticism. "Surely, if he wrote books, there must be copies of them---somewhere. And if he pastored a church, there surely must be records of that also---some kind, somewhere!"

Sadly he shook his head, affirming his original statement, and said, "None! I have looked, but all I could find was one book!" he declared, as he pulled it out of his briefcase and handed it to me. "No church records, no publishing records, and no other books, that I could find!"

"Well, then, how do you know all about him and the books, if you have never seen any records of him, or any books by him but this one?" I asked again.

"My father told me about him, but that will take some explanation also. You see, my mother died at childbirth, so I never knew her. I was adopted as a baby into a fine Christian home, and never knew my birth father till about five months ago. He called one day and asked if he could see me. I agreed, and after showing me proof that he was my father, he told me of the family background of the Sangsters. My great-great-grandfather, William Sangster, was a preacher, and he pastored the same church up in the North Carolina mountains for forty-three years. He was a prolific writer and a powerful preacher. Some of his books were published, though my father didn't know how many."

"Do you mean that none of them survived?" I asked.

"To our knowledge just one or two! But the worst part is that his record of existence in the small town in the mountains, where he pastored, hasn't survived either. My father went there, not long ago, to try to find records at the city library and then at the church, but it's as if he had never existed. Dr. Pointer, why would someone want to wipe out the memory and even the record of the existence of a man of God, especially someone so loved, so my father tells me, by the people he pastored for so long? Well, anyway, my father not only found no record, but he met strong resistance to his efforts and questions, as he sought to gain any kind of information about William Sangster."

"Well, now, you do have a number of problems!" I asserted, speaking of his dissertation primarily. "First, is such a man a significant figure that he would be worthy of a dissertation? You would need to prove that first, before you could write on some area of his theology. Second, what about sources? Obviously, you could not write on a man without the sources---his books in this case. Third, would there be the possibility that you would be too close to this man emotionally to write objectively on his view or views of theology? I am not saying a dissertation on him is impossible, but surely you can see the problems."

He acknowledged that he had counted not only the cost, but he had noted the very problems I had mentioned. Then he handed me the following list of names and dates, beginning with the man whose theology he hoped to pursue in a doctoral dissertation.

1.	William Sangster	1870-1943
2.	William Sangster, Jr.	1892-1962
3.	William Sangster, III	1915-1980
4.	William Sangster IV	1941-
5.	William Sangster V	1960-

I must say my curiosity had been aroused! My mind too was filled with questions over this strange mystery! Not that I was unaccustomed to mysteries. I warned him that even after much work of investigation and research into this man and his writings, the result might very well be that we would come up empty, thus no dissertation. He acknowledged that did not concern him, as finding the truth was his primary goal. I asked him to give me a few days to think about the matter, before saying anything positive or negative about the possibility of a dissertation on William Sangster.

After he had left, I called Dink to tell him of this strange mystery. He admitted that he had never heard anything like it before either, and he agreed to help me with any investigation of this unique and unexplainable historical disappearance of the original William Sangster. He even suggested that we take a trip to this little town of Comptonville, where Sangster had pastored for forty-three years, and see what we could find. He did warn me that it could be dangerous, because if someone had gone to so much trouble to get rid of the historical record of this man, they must have had a good reason, or in this case a strong bad reason. This surely meant that they would not relish someone snooping around to uncover the mystery they had created---which now had been hidden for so many years.

I thought to myself, what's new? We've been there before! But I could never anticipate the difficulty or the danger of our coming search!

3 Where Is Comptonville?

After talking with Dink, I picked up the copy of the William Sangster book, which the great-great-grandson had left with me. As I browsed through it, and then read parts of it, I was very impressed. This man was an unusually gifted writer. Many commentaries do not know the balance between the devotional and the scholarly. They are either warm and fuzzy and filled with devotional thoughts, or dry and scholarly with little insight into the real life setting and application of a passage. William Sangster was a man who knew how to balance both the scholarly and the practical. I was even more convinced of the need to do all we could to unravel the mystery of this godly and gifted man.

Thus the early morning of the next day found Dink and me on the road, not knowing what to expect when we got to Comptonville, if we could even find the place. All went fairly normal in our travel, until we left the main highway, which we had taken up into the mountains, which itself was a rather remote roadway. The route back into the small city of Comptonville was a winding, bumpy highway, if you could call it even a highway, with a few houses scattered along the way. Probably, only God knew how many other houses were scattered back in the mountains, up or down some of the very difficult side roads, which led from our main route. One could tell by the type of homes that the people were not anywhere near the middle class. We passed only a few cars, as it was one of the most deserted roads I had ever traveled.

Then, suddenly, we popped over a hill, and there below in the valley was what had to be Comptonville. I must say, that even from our perch up above the town, I was taken back by one of the buildings in the center of the little city, which stuck out like a sore thumb. It appeared from this distance to be a church---a large, beautiful, magnificent building, which seemed totally out of place in a community like Comptonville. How on earth had such a poor community been able to build such an edifice and why?

As we drove down the hill into the town, we couldn't help but notice that the homes were still very humble ones, the automobiles were rather old, and most of the people were in the range of senior citizens. Very few children were evident, even at the school complex. I looked at Dink and he looked at me, but neither of us said anything, except we both shook our heads from the surprise. This was a very unusual little town---but why and how? Then as we reached the middle of the city, just driving through to see where the library was, a police car began to follow us. Then the light on the police car began to twirl, signifying that we had better pull over.

"You boys got business here in Comptonville?" one of the officers asked.

"We just wanted to visit the library!" I replied.

"Ain't they got no libaries where you come from?" he said slowly, seeming to rebuke us for even being in town.

"Is it a law for someone to visit the library?" I asked in response.

"No, can't say that it is. But get your business done, and leave town as soon as possible. We're gonna have our eyes pinned on you boys, as long as you're here!" he warned.

We parked and went into the library, and almost every eye was raised as we entered. I looked for the card catalogue and made a beeline for it, before someone could stop me. Quickly, I turned to "Sangster," thinking surely I would find his books in the city library. But there were no books written by any "William Sangster" listed there.

Almost immediately, I was approached by an elderly woman, who came at me from behind the desk. She asked with some suspicion, "Are you looking for something?"

"Yes!" I answered, wondering what purpose she thought a library served. "I am looking to see if you have the works of William Sangster in your library, a man who pastored here for forty-three years back some while ago."

Coldly she replied, "No, he didn't write any books! Sorry! Now you had better leave!" Then she turned to walk back to her desk.

As I followed her, I asked. "But wasn't he pastor of the First Baptist Church for forty-three years from 1900-1943?"

She stopped so quickly that I almost ran over her, and with a cold bluntness of voice and a look of scorn, she said, "Leave, before I call the police!"

As we left, I was certain she was calling the police. Dink met me at the door, as he had been looking around the library on his own. I took a peak over my shoulder, as I moved toward the car, and noticed the rude lady was watching me to see where I might go next. After we were out of her sight, we made another beeline for the First Baptist Church, wondering now how long it would be before the police found us. Surely, the First Baptist Church would have a record of his pastorate there! Or would they?

As we drove, Dink said, "Preacha, I don't like dis! We could disappear out here, an nobody, an' I means nobody, would ever hear of us again or have any idea of what happened ta us! Da sooner we's gets outta here, da better! Dis place scares me!"

That was quite a statement coming from Dink, in light of his years as a leader in the gang world, whereby he had seen all kinds of danger. But I convinced him that we needed to check the church before we left, and we did. We found a side door open with a hallway containing pictures of the pastors of the church, going all the way back to the church's beginning. But when we came to 1900-1943, there was the picture of another man named Samuel Newell hanging on the wall in the place of William Sangster.

About this time the doors we had entered opened, and our two policemen friends came running through the doors with guns drawn, and the spokesman informed us, "Hey, dontcha know that you boys is a trespassin' on private property?"

"Sorry, sir, but we thought a church was public property. It is where we come from."

"Well, this ain't the big city. We have to watch outsiders carefully, because they steal things, you know! So this ain't private property to you boys---especially during a weekday. How can we know what kind of mischief you're up to here? Now I'm gonna ask you boys to leave town once more, or else I'm gonna take you to the hoos-gow. Take your pick---leave town or jail. And if you ever come back again, it will be jail for sure! So don't get any further ideas about snooping around here in Comptonville!"

Since he didn't give us really much of a choice, and since we didn't want to find out where or what the hoos-gow was, we promised to leave town. Their guns were still on us as we walked gingerly past them, not knowing exactly what to expect. They followed us to our car, and then several miles past the city limits, before they turned back. We noticed, as we passed through the mountains, several other police cars from small communities were waiting for us and gave us an escort through their fair cities.

Finally, Dink said wonderingly, "Sure too bad we didn't get da chance ta check da grave yard! He's gots ta be buried somewhere! But I don't wants ta know dat bad enough ta go back."

We both agreed that there were many other questions that needed answers. Who gave all the money to build such a magnificent church? Someone has or has had at one time some wealth in that town. And it seems clear that someone is pulling the puppet strings manipulating the whole town in this mystery of deceit and intrigue! Someone who was even willing to kill for it?

"Kinda scary, ain't it!" Dink offered!

4 Is This an Impossible Situation?

As we were riding home, I came to the conclusion that we were now in an impossible situation. I asked myself how the Lord was going to solve this problem. I saw no human explanation or possibility whereby He would or could solve this mystery. That doesn't mean that I felt He could not and would not solve it, but that humanly speaking, there was no way I could see. I shared with Dink that we needed to begin a study of the Bible, considering impossible situations, which God solved by His power.

Then another question came to me. Could this seemingly impossible situation compare with the major Biblical events, where God displayed such omnipotence to turn the tide against a seemingly unsolvable and impossible situation, which He had allowed the great enemy to create within His divine purpose and plan? I concluded, yes, because God tells me in His word that all Scripture is given by the inspiration of God and is profitable for doctrine, for reproof, for correction, and for instruction in righteousness, that I might be completely furnished for every good work (II Timothy 3:16ff). This was a good work, and I needed instruction, and God's word about men in similar situations could be looked upon as instructions for me, even though their situations were recorded in the Bible and mine were not. Yet, the Word of God equally applies to both.

I turned on the dome light so I could see my Bible, and asked Dink if it bothered him as he drove. His reply was clear as he said, "Not if what youse is goin' ta say is gonna feed my soul wid encouragement!"

I had two books with me---my Bible and a book by one of my favorite devotional writers on the Pentateuch. So I turned in my Bible to Genesis 6, which contains the beginning of the story of Noah and the flood. This was a passage, which presented to Noah an impossible situation for himself and his family. True, he had found grace in the eyes of the Lord, but he may well have wondered what good that would do, when God had announced that He was going to destroy all flesh, because the earth was filled with violence (see Genesis 6:13). God's Spirit would no longer strive with man. God would destroy man from the face of the earth! All creatures of His creation would soon be gone from His earth.

Was this good news for Noah? Not hardly! For God's original statement seemed to include the destruction of all mankind, including Noah! God had said, "All flesh shall be destroyed! I will destroy man whom I have created from the face of the earth!" What a consternation of confusion and concern this must have initially brought to Noah, when he first heard those words---all flesh shall be destroyed!

But soon God spoke further words, which should have been somewhat encouraging to Noah, but which certainly did not immediately solve his dilemma nor remove all his concerns. God told him to build an ark of gopher wood (see Genesis 6:14ff), giving him the dimensions of three hundred cubits in length, fifty cubits wide, and thirty cubits high. Taking a cubit to be eighteen inches in length, the ark would be 450 feet long, 75 feet wide, and 45 feet high. God gave further instructions for building the ark, and then spoke of His covenant with Noah. Again, I wondered if that promise melted all Noah's confusion, though it should have. But even yet, questions could and must have still been ringing in his mind?

"God, what's an ark? I have never seen such a thing before! Where is all the water coming from to float a thing that big? What is rain? Can enough of that rain stuff come to float the ark in just 40 days and 40 nights?"

Had Noah ever seen rain before? And what did he know about water and buoyancy? What would keep such a large piece of wood afloat (many pieces of wood, actually), especially, when it would be loaded with animals and his family and provisions? Could he even imagine such a structure one and one half times the size of a modern football field in length?

In reality Scripture mentions nothing of this kind of doubting or questioning, though it mentions fear. It summarizes the whole situation in Hebrews 11:7:

> By faith, Noah being warned of God of things not seen as yet, moved with fear, prepared an ark to the saving of his house, by which he condemned the world, and became heir of the righteousness which is by faith.

Surely, this was an impossible situation, but the answer was faith in God and His promises, which being a true faith, moved in obedience to obey God's commands. And so it will ever be with those given faith by God! True faith is not a hope or a pleasant desire fostered by man until the tempests come. True faith faces the storms of life, as harsh and as stern as they may be, with a never surrendering conviction of God's faithfulness! Faith then rides through the storm as commanded, and lives to see the day of God's victory in accordance with His promise and purpose.

So it was with Noah, and so it will be with us, as we possess and exercise our true God-given faith in our Lord Jesus Christ. But, it will not be so with the professing worldling, who has a false faith, which seems to shine in the days of ease and comfort, only to wilt as a fading flower in the flaming heat of the noon day sun.

I quoted some thoughts from the book I was carrying, as the author commented on this passage.

> But oh, those solemn words, "I will destroy!" What a heavy gloom they would cast over the glittering scene. Could not man's genius invent some way of escape? Could not "the mighty man deliver himself by his strength?" Alas! No. There was one way of escape, but it was revealed to faith, not sight, not to reason, not to imagination. (Mackintosh, *Genesis to Deuteronomy,* p. 47)

> Nature is governed by what it sees,--it is governed by its senses. Faith is governed by the pure Word of God (inestimable treasure in this dark world!); this gives stability, let outward appearances be what they may. (Mackintosh, p. 47)

> A single line of sacred Scripture is an abundant answer to all the reasonings and all the imaginations of the human mind; and when one has the Word of God as the basis of his convictions, he may calmly stand against the full tide of human opinion and prejudice. (Mackintosh, p. 48)

5 Shall We Go Back to Comptonville?

It was the early morning darkness which finally welcomed us back to Seminary City. After a few hours with my family members, who were just rising for the activities of the day, I dashed my face with cold water, and headed to school for an early appointment with William Sangster. I could hardly wait to share with him our experiences in Comptonville. When I told him the whole story of our trials in that fair city, it didn't seem to dampen his spirit one bit, concerning writing of his thesis on William Sangster's theology.

He came on strong when I was finished, as he said, "Dr. Pointer, this surely shows us that something very wrong has and is still going on there. Though my father has known about this for several months, he has not been able to do anything about it. He ran into the same threats you did. Which raises the question, how can we gather information with such threats and restrictions placed upon us? We need information, but the information seems to be found in Comptonville only, and we are shut out of that city now!"

I encouraged him to have faith, and then I shared with him my midnight study with Dink on Noah, as we had traveled home, which seemed to encourage him. He even asked if he could be part of the study of further passages, which taught the display of God's omnipotence in other impossible situations. I agreed, but said I might have to share with him sometimes separately, after I had met with Dink. I noted that it was going to be very difficult for us to meet from time to time, especially if we made progress in finding who was at the heart of the problem in Comptonville. He said he understood that.

As we parted, it was obvious that we both were more eager than ever for him to write his thesis on William Sangster, if at all possible. There was not only a theology to be pursued in Sangster's writings, but also a story to be told concerning his life, and then his historical erasure from the city, where he had ministered for so many years.

It was about this time that the Lord brought to my mind Mac Turnover and his Turnover News Agency, a man who had been saved in our previous ministry. (Belcher, *A Journey in Inspiration*) He certainly had the contacts to get information that was not available to us. But then after calling Mac, and telling him the story of William Sangster and our experiences in Comptonville, he reported back to me several hours later that he had hit nothing but a dead end in his attempt to find anything about a William Sangster. He asked if I was positive he had lived in Comptonville during the dates I had given him. I think this fact challenged him even more, as he saw a story, even a gigantic story, if we could find a crack in the door to enter the town for research concerning the man and the town.

He raised the question of someone going back into Comptonville. Would they really carry out their threats in the face of a national news agency lurking there? Surely the answer to that question depended on how high the stakes were in the game they were playing. Could the stakes be as high as death to keep someone from uncovering their little dirty secret, whatever it was?

But who should go? Dink and I? Mac and his investigators? A single investigator posing as a man seeking work? But was it really safe for anyone to go back until we knew more about the whole situation?

How we needed the Lord's guidance in these matters, though, before we did anything!

6 How Did Joseph React to the His Trial?

A few days later Dink and I met to study one of my favorite Bible characters. If there was ever a man who was shut in by an impossible situation, it was Joseph of the Old Testament. Loved by his father, but misunderstood and hated by his older brothers, because of his godliness and spiritual gifts, he must have wondered what God was doing, when he was sold into slavery. Can one even begin to imagine the consternation of his heart, when his brothers did such a thing? Then what grief in his soul he must have experienced, as he traveled past his own home area on his way as a slave to Egypt, unknown to his father, who may have been just a little ways from the main road he traveled.

But then, after languishing in prison for a long while, he was bought out of slavery by Potiphar, an officer of Pharaoh, captain of the guard. When his master saw that the Lord was with him, and all that he did was made to prosper, he made him the master of his house. The blessing of the Lord was upon all in Potiphar's house because of Joseph. Surely, Joseph rejoiced over God's blessings, and probably never anticipated that he would go back to prison.

But he did, when he resisted Potiphar's wife's advances, and the result was that he was falsely accused of the same towards her. So back to prison it was to start at the bottom of the ladder again, where he had been just recently for such a long time. Did he ask God what He was doing? Did he ask God why this had come to pass? Did he not, perhaps, face the same temptation we do---to question God and His dealings with him? Nonetheless, there he languished in prison for a number of years, with neither human hope nor human power to help him---only faith in his God and His power to deliver him from the bondage of prison and death there. Talk about an impossible situation ---this was it, humanly speaking.

But, then, in the unfolding of God's sovereign plan, which was unknown to Joseph, he found favor once again by interpreting dreams, even Pharaoh's dream. And to the surprise of all, maybe even himself, he was exalted to be the second person in power under Pharaoh in Egypt. God, again in His providence, was using all the above seemingly impossible situation, to bring His people down to Egypt, where they could multiply for over 400 years, before He would move them back to the Promised Land. God's plan for His people for years to come was being worked out in all the unexplainable and tragic events in the life of this one man Joseph.

After stating my thoughts, I shared some thoughts of our author, whom we had used previously. These quotes come not from his comments on Joseph in his consideration of Genesis, but from another source, as he spoke of the absolute necessity of obedience to God in every situation. They are applicable to us, as we seek to walk in obedience to God in an impossible hour of testing.

> They (the words of God in the Bible) teach us that it is better, if it must be so, to stand, like a marble statue, on the pathway of obedience, than to reach the most desirable ends by transgressing a plain precept of the Word of God. (C. H. Mackintosh, *The Mackintosh Treasury*, p. 19)

> May we not be found looking askance to catch the approving look of a poor mortal whose breath is in his nostrils, nor sigh to find our names amid the glittering record of the great men of the age. The servant of

> Christ should look far beyond all such things. The grand business of the servant is to obey. His object should not be to do a great deal, but simply to do what he is told. (Mackintosh, p. 19)

I would remind us that Joseph did all of this without compromising his life or the Word of God. How easy it is to compromise the truth of God, in order to help ourselves (we think) get out from under the bondage of a boxed-in situation. Our author speaks to this attitude as well, though again, not specifically in the context of a discussion of Joseph. Yet it applies to Joseph in his life and struggles and trials.

> We therefore hold it nothing short of positive blasphemy to assert that we have arrived in a stage of our career in which the Bible (the Word of God) is not sufficient, or that we are compelled to travel outside its covers to find ample guidance and instruction for the present moment, and every moment of our earthly pilgrimage.... We do not want tradition to assist revelation, but we use revelation as the test of tradition. We should just as soon think of bringing out a rush light to assist the sun's meridian beams, as of calling in human tradition to aid divine revelation. (Mackintosh, p. 18)

It must be admitted that Joseph did not have a Bible, but that is not to say he had no revelation of God. It is quite clear that he walked not in accordance with the wisdom or traditions of men, but he trusted the word of God, and such faith in God's word will never fail the child of God today.

7 Where Shall We Turn for Help?

At the close of our study, we had to admit that it was God, and undeniably God, Who had brought both of these men from their seemingly impossible circumstances---Noah from the danger of death in the flood and Joseph from the pit of death in the dungeon. Who could deny that fact? God did it for there was no hope for either man in those dismal hours of their lives!

Thus we prayed that we would be faithful as well in our hour of testing in the matter before us. We did want to be responsible to our duty, whatever that might be, but we wanted all to know that if there was ever to be a victory, it would be of God and not of our plans or human power. As we prayed these things, I was aware of the click in the slot in my office door, which signaled the deliverance of the morning mail, though I thought nothing of it at this hour, for it was a very normal thing.

But when we had finished praying, as Dink and I continued talking, I slipped over to the door to check the mail. To my surprise there was one letter with no stamp on it and no return address. When I opened it, I found the following message:

> If you value your life, you will never return to Comptonville again. This goes for anyone you might send!

I showed the talkative Dink the note, and he was silent for a few minutes after reading it. My mind began to wonder out loud who we might contact to help us with this? Not the Comptonville police force, obviously. Not any of the police surrounding the city of Comptonville. Not the state's attorney---not enough evidence. Not the FBI for the same reason, plus they probably would be reluctant to meddle in such a small town's problems, if such problems could ever be proven. We concluded once again that the dead end was a reality all right. We needed a work of God to break the log-jam. But how? And when? And what could we do in the meantime, but wait?

After Dink had left my office, I picked up the one volume of William Sangster's works that I had, and began to read it again. What an uplifting and godly book! It was a commentary on Psalms. What insight and ability of expression. Each chapter and every paragraph caused the reader to pause and meditate on the points of the author's discussion. I concluded again that it was more than a commentary. It was a devotional commentary, done not only with insight into the original language and practices of the people of the Biblical author's day, but there was application of these precious truths to the hearts of believers today.

I had read many commentaries in my day, but none quite like this one! I was more determined than ever to find the remainder of William Sangster's works, so they could benefit Christians of our day. The only remaining questions were who had sought to hide them from the public, and when, and why. Plus, the obvious question remained---how could we find them? Only by faith in God's omnipotent power!

8 Does Anyone Care in Comptonville?

My thoughts were interrupted by a phone call from Mac, as he wanted to talk to me about the Sangster situation. He sought my reaction to the idea of sending one of his investigators into Comptonville to see what he could find. I tried to discourage him, because of the danger, and then I read him the brief note we had received that very morning. But that didn't seem to discourage him, even though I warned him of the possible results. His answer was that every good reporter takes risks to get a story, and my reply was that we shouldn't tempt God. I had to admit that it was quite a story, but was it worth the risk?

I suggested he bring in a reporter, but not to Comptonville. Why not check the state's denominational records or the Baptist state newspaper's records. Surely, one or both of these would have had some record, and maybe even an article on such a long ministry in one place. And what about the local Baptist association (wherever it was located, and hopefully not in Comptonville)? How about trying to check other relatives, who lived outside of Comptonville? Why face the lion head on, when we could attack him indirectly somehow?

He agreed those were good ideas, and maybe it would be better to take my suggested approach, although his reporter's heart wanted a quick and direct shot at the story. He noted that he would send someone to these mentioned Baptist avenues of information very soon, and he would let me know the results. Then, if necessary, he would send someone into Comptonville.

I had hardly hung up the phone, when it rang again. The voice on the other end of the line was husky, probably on purpose, in order to disguise the caller's identity.

"Dr. Pointer, please, do not give up your pursuit of the Comptonville scandal!" a voice challenged me. "You are my only hope! I'll be there for you when you need me!"

I stood there for a moment, hoping to ask some questions, but he was gone. Then I tried to remember his exact words, and I turned immediately to write them down. I read them several times to see what conclusions I could draw from them. I listed several possibilities:

1. Comptonville has a scandal!
2. One man was behind us in our search for the truth.
3. This man was watching the developments and us.
4. This man would back us at a certain point in time.
5. This man was probably in danger himself.
6. This man would still help at a certain point.
7. This man must know the full story of the scandal.
8. This man wanted the scandal brought to light

I had to admit that this person was an encouragement to me. How many more were silent observers, hoping for someone to come and deliver them from the bondage of the past years and expose whoever was under the covers of the cover-up?

I concluded that God was at work and in His time the scandal and the scandaler (my new word) would be brought to justice. In God's time---we could not force it! May God give us patience to wait on Him in order to see His great power bring this all to a conclusion. By faith we press on!

9 How Long Will It Take God to Move?

The next few days were a weekend, and I was glad. I spent some time with the family, some time resting, and some hours preaching the Word of God to others. Then the first thing Monday morning found us back on the trail of the scandal in Comptonville, but not without our study of the Word of God. We had moved to consider Moses now, and God's deliverance of His people from Egypt.

It seems clear that God's people were in good standing in Egypt for over 400 years, until there arose a king in Egypt, who knew not Joseph. In simple words the memory of Joseph and his contributions, as well as the contribution of God's people, was forgotten, after many years of their living in peace in that foreign land. This new Pharaoh feared the multiplication of these foreigners, lest they come to outnumber the Egyptians, and join Egypt's enemies to fight against them. Therefore, they had to be enslaved and cut down in their population, and thus Pharaoh thought he could deal with God's people without any problem whatsoever by eliminating children at birth!

God's people at this point seemed to be shut up with no ability to help themselves escape the wrath and power of this Egyptian tyrant, who thought it was his calling to reduce their number any way he could. So there came the wrath of Pharaoh, as he put over God's people the stern and ruthless taskmasters, who demanded impossible hours of work and labor, which brought to God's people greater burdens, bondage and enslavement. What hope did this foreign people have, though they were great in number, in defeating the power and armies of Pharaoh in his unrestricted desires and efforts to control them in accordance with his whims and desires?

From this attitude of Pharaoh came the edict that every Jewish son born was to be thrown into the river, which river quickly became the place of death for many a Jewish child. But then there came a hope! God gave a deliverer named Moses. Saved from death by Pharaoh's daughter, reared under the nose of Pharaoh himself in his very palace, trained in the best of the universities of Egypt, and no doubt, skilled in the way of military battle and strategy. Yet all of this was unknown to the Jewish nation itself, as God was working quietly to raise up a deliver, even while the situation in Egypt deteriorated, as far as the plight of the people themselves. Again, I say, this was all unknown to the Jewish nation, who saw no hope for the future!

Then the hour came, so Moses thought, when he was forty years old. He was God's deliverer! He came forth valiantly to take a stand for the people of God by killing a cruel taskmaster. But his efforts failed, as God's people did not trust him in his actions, and Moses had to flee Egypt for fear of Pharaoh himself. Surely, the plight of the nation of Israel became even more impossible, when their unknown but hoped for deliverer fled Egypt and went to live on the backside of the Midian desert, tending sheep, probably with no thoughts or hopes of ever seeking to be their deliverer again. Had not the Jewish people been boxed in hopelessly prior to Moses' efforts to deliver them? And does this not make their deliverance to the human mind even more impossible? Surely, they had questions. Where is our God? Why does He not show Himself? Has He not failed us! Is not our situation absolutely hopeless and undeniably beyond human help?

In all reality would you or I have given them any hope, had we been there and didn't know the outcome which was to come? Is it not true that the human heart and the human eye often cannot see the way that God is moving? But does that mean He will not move to deliver His people from the brutality of the taskmasters, which assail us? So we cry and moan and conclude the situation surely is beyond even the power and ability of God to help us. Or if it isn't, for some reason He has chosen not to help us, and this stirs the question as to why not? Why does God wait so long? Why doesn't He do something now? Anything, but do it now! Thus we want to dictate to God the time and the place and the means of our deliverance from a trial or heartache! And if He does not comply with our blueprint and timetable, He must not love us, or He has forgotten us, or He is not able to defeat the enemy, or this, or that, or whatever comes into our struggling minds of unbelief.

But is it not true that God had painted the children of Israel into a corner, so that when the deliverance came, no one, and I mean no one, could say, look what man did? Is that not what man is prone to do---to take the credit for what God has done? If deliverance from a trial came easy, and if we could develop a plan for our deliverance, would we not then take the credit, instead of giving the glory to God? How gracious of God to teach us, even through trials, that He is the power of deliverance, and not we ourselves. And we will only see this, when we are in a position of helplessness with no possibility of dependence upon ourselves for our deliverance. Just once wouldn't you like to see God get the glory, when He moves by His power in an impossible situation?

Maybe that is the reason He paints us into that corner, where there is no human hope, no human help, no human power, no human plan, no human scheme, whereby we can extricate ourselves. And when we are delivered, we can only give Him the glory, as we say, "Look what God did!"

Maybe that is the reason He allows us to stay in that trial or endure in length that hardship, so that when the deliverance comes we will long remember that which was burned into our brain during those lonely hours of despair. That the situation was hopeless---until God…!

Maybe that is the reason He allows us to lie in our pain and uncertainty at times, when it seems so pointless to us? He wants us to get the message that He is the omnipotent God, and we must give Him the glory for our deliverance, when it comes. May God spare us from seeking to take His glory in any manner, when our deliverance comes!

I looked at Dink for any comments, as I spoke, and he could only shake his head.

"We sure better be careful dat we has da mind of da Lord before we do sometin' in dis Comptonville ting. It sure looks hopeless now, but ain't it been hopeless fer many years? Hasn't several generations suffered from dis scandal? Sounds a little bit like da children of Israel---not as many people, not on da front page in God's plan of da ages, but people sufferin' and still sufferin' in a hopeless situation, wid no one ta help dem but God."

I could only agree with him, so we prayed for guidance in what we were to do, realizing things could get worse before they got better. Were we really ready for that, especially if it included us?

10 Any Ideas on What's Going On In Comptonville?

It was a Tuesday, when I finally heard from Mac again. He informed me that the local Baptist association had no record of William Sangster, nor did the several adjoining associations. The local group's building had burned back in 1952, so that was the reason for a lack of full records. But the attempt to restore accurate records from the local churches, showed no record of William Sangster either. Yet the Baptist state convention office did have records of him in fullness. He was an author, a denominational statesman, a theologian, a strong leader, a sound conservative scholar, and a prolific writer, according to their description.

I told Mac about the mysterious caller, who said he was behind us, and he seemed encouraged to know someone was with us. When I asked him about his next move, if any, he said he would send in a reporter very soon, because this story was too big to ignore. Injustice seems to have been done to a very godly man, to say nothing of the disservice to the church and its people. Then, he told me it would be my friend Phil Scott, the man who had helped us in one of our recent journeys, when Dink was missing, and we were trying to find him. (Belcher, *A Journey in Roman Catholicism*) He told me also that Phil was now a Christian, after seeing our faith in the matter with Dink, as he worked with us.

I rejoiced with him over the fact of Phil's salvation, and then I informed him that Dink and I didn't see any reason for us to go into Comptonville again, and he agreed that was a good decision. They would probably be waiting for us, and who knows what could happen. Phil would at least be a new face, and it might take them awhile to get onto his purpose there.

By the time I got off the phone, I felt again like my mind was caught in a whirlwind of thoughts and questions concerning this whole matter. It seemed so unreal! Was it possible that forty plus years of a man's life could be erased from history in light of the fact that he had lived it in the presence of so many other people and left such an impact by his life? I could see how an insignificant unknown man could be swallowed up by a community (though that too would be difficult), but a man of the magnitude of importance and influence of a William Sangster? What about his family? How could they ever let something like that happen?

How could the public records be cleansed of the name of William Sangster and his family? William, my student, had informed me that there were no birth records, no death certificates, and no grave records. There was no tombstone or burial plot with the name of William Sangster written on it. It's as if he had never lived!

As William had explained to me, the whole matter was dormant for years, as all the Sangsters and their kin had been driven out of the community and had scattered far and wide, even seeking anonymity. The records, and even the cemeteries, were purged of all remembrances of the Sangster family, and whoever was behind it felt satisfied the matter was settled. But had anyone ever come around asking questions, and if so, what had happened to them?

I must confess that last question sent chills up and down my spine. Were Dink and I the only ones who had ever visited the place and lived to tell it? That thought made me glad we were not going back to Comptonville---ever! So I thought!

11 How Long Since We Have Said, Look What God Did?

About this time Dink walked in and wanted to look at the further life of Moses in relation to our study. We had left Moses in the desert, where he had gone when he was forty years old, after the people of God rejected him to be their deliverer. We picked him up in our meditations in Exodus 3, where he was now eighty years old.

That means that for forty years his burden to be Israel's deliverer from Egypt had lain dormant, and was now, humanly speaking, considered to be impossible. It was dead! Who would call or use an eighty-year-old man to lead two million people out of such a dangerous place as Egypt? No doubt he sat many afternoons, watching his flocks in the shade, thinking of what could have been, and wondering why it had not been.

Had he made a mistake to think God's call was upon him to lead His people out of Egypt? Had he made a mistake in trying to do the job too soon, when he killed the Egyptian taskmaster? Did he wonder about his immaturity at forty, as the maturity of eighty approached? Dare he dream that God's call was still to come? Did that dream begin to fade the older he became, until it was finally all but a broken memory in his broken heart? But worst of all, were God's people destined to spend hundreds of years more in Egypt, rather than in their Promised Land? And what had happened to God's promise to Abraham, Isaac and Jacob? Was there a better prospect that God was raising up to be the deliver---a better prospect than he had been when he was forty?

And then God's call came to him, and Moses could only ask who he was that he should go and lead this people out of Egypt! His questions are understandable! I don't even know God's name! Who shall I say sent me? They will not believe me! They will not listen to my voice! They will say the Lord has not appeared unto you! I am not eloquent! I am slow of speech! I am slow of tongue!

Can we not understand his objections---objections that had grown in his mind for forty years, as the result of a festering heart. Can we not understand his probable human conclusions that God had not called him and would never call him to lead His people from Egypt! Objections come easy and in great number, when one has had forty years to analyze a situation in unbelief from every angle, and then draw parallel false conclusions.

All of this negativity was surely present, even in light of all that God said and did to encourage him at this hour, during the renewed call for him to go as God's deliverer. There was the flaming fire coming forth from a bush, which did not burn! There was God's command to take off his shoes, for he stood on holy ground! There was the clear identification of God as the speaker---the God of Abraham, and Isaac, and Jacob! There was the statement from God that this was the time of deliverance! There was God's command to behold the cry of the children of Israel! There was the news that God would send him forth to Pharaoh to bring His people out of Egypt! There was the promise that God would be with him! There was the promise that God's people would listen to him! There was the promise that God would smite Egypt! Yet still Moses was reluctant to go! Why, one might ask?

Was it not that the children of Israel were boxed in without hope of ever leaving Egypt? If they were to come out, which seemed impossible at this moment, it would take a young man of faith, Moses may have supposed, and not an eighty-year-old shepherd, who was well past his prime. Yet, was there not in the back of Moses heart and mind a desire to be that deliverer? Was there not a dormant faith, which had once burned fiercely with hope and certainty that God could do it? Was it not that God simply had to rekindle that flame of conviction, which once had burned by faith that God would do as He promised?

Was it not faith, which had caused him at a young age, (and what a faith it was), when he was called the son of Pharaoh's daughter, to turn his back on Egypt, and choose rather to suffer affliction with the people of God, rather than to enjoy the pleasures of sin for a season?

Was it not faith. which had caused him to esteem the reproach of Christ to be of greater riches than all the treasures in Egypt, as he saw and choose the great spiritual reward of serving God, rather than the spoils of Egypt?

Was it not faith which caused him to forsake Egypt, not fearing the wrath of Pharaoh, as he endured it all by seeing the One Who is invisible, rather than centering on the visible things of this world?

Truly the faith was there, but it needed to be stirred and revived and renewed! And it was rekindled, as Moses obeyed God, as God commanded him to go and to do the work to which God had called him! Did he not know that he must suffer the hardships God had called him to face, and to lead this people out of the land of Egypt, as God had commanded?

How often does our faith lie dormant for years, when it had been strong earlier in life? How often do we make excuses about the future, because of the disappointments and failures of the past, which failures may have been the literal training ground of God for a moment for us to serve Him in the future for His greater glory?

Is it not true that past disappointments may have been part of God's preparation for a greater future for His glory? Could there ever have been the Moses we know in victory at eighty, without the Moses we know in defeat at forty? Had not God boxed in Moses and the children of Israel for forty years to show them that when the deliverance came, it was not of Moses or Aaron or any other man, but of God?

Is not God glorified in a greater manner, when we face a death situation, than when we face the normal living of our lives, where we feel we can handle everything on our own? Does not God specialize in death situations and boxed in moments in the life of His people? Does He not allow the enemy a greater sway to do his utmost against us, so that he can paint God's people into an impossible corner, so God can show His full power to His people? Is it not then that we know that He is God---there is none like Him?

Will we ever learn that God's purpose is to glorify Himself in our midst, not to glorify us or our abilities or our wisdom or our talent or our power---that it is His name that He seeks to exalt, not ours? And is not that only possible when all earthly hopes, and human powers, and human wisdom, and human plans, and human schemes have failed ---when God's people know that their only hope is God, and they cry out in despair, as did the children of Israel?

Yes, God prepared Israel, as he brought them to despair and hopelessness, and God prepared Moses, as He brought him to the end of himself and his power! Then God moved by His power for His glory alone---so all the world would know and say, "Look what God did!"

How long has it been since you and I have said with joy and highest exaltation after facing an hour of hopelessness and despair, "Look what God did!"

12 What Is Our Next Step?

After Dink left, I decided to do some work on a new course on Romans, which I was to teach in the coming fall semester. I had already gone through the book of Romans with a Greek method I used, and had drawn many insights and clear conclusions, along with the preparation of the outline of the whole book. I now was going to add to my notes some ideas from several commentaries, which I had obtained, but which had been previously unused in any depth.

Thus I began to read the introductory material in one commentary, and then I plunged into the author's discussion of the text of the Scriptures. I had not read hardly a page or two, when something struck me about the style of this author. The style and language were amazingly similar to the commentary I had read by William Sangster on Psalms! Could it be that this was William Sangster's work on Romans, which had sat on my shelf for several months, and I hadn't even noticed it?

Quickly, I flipped back to the title page and read the name of the author---Clark Compton. I knew of this author, as he was the president of the largest seminary of our denomination. But that was about all I knew about him. So I turned to the dust jacket, which contained his picture and some biographical information.

He was from a wealthy Southern family and was educated at the seminary where he now served as president. Early in his ministry as a teacher, he had shown promise as a commentator and scholar by the impact of his teaching and the productivity of his pen, writing commentaries on many of the major books of the Bible, including Genesis, Romans, Luke, Psalms, and many others.

The mention of the last book, Psalms, stopped me in my tracks! Psalms---a commentary on Psalms! Dare I compare Compton's commentary on Psalms with the book on my shelf---William Sangster's work on Psalms? Their styles were so similar! Could it be possible that Compton had plagiarized William Sangster's work, and then thought it necessary to eliminate the memory of Sangster to keep anyone from discovering and revealing his deception?

And then came another question, and I wondered why I hadn't seen this question immediately. What about his name--Compton? Could his home town be Comptonville, and could his family's wealth and influence in that city have been the force and power behind the obliteration of the work and name of William Sangster from the town records, in order to cover up Clark Compton's plagiarism?

I made several phone calls to fellow professors, who I hoped would be on campus today, to see if any of them had a copy of Compton's work on Psalms. Several calls were no answers, and several more were negatives---they didn't have that book. But, finally, Bill Sawyers, an Old Testament professor, was in his office, and he had a copy of Compton on the Psalms. I literally ran across campus to his office, secured the book, and began to read it, as I walked slowly back to my office. I didn't have Sangster's book with me, but I immediately saw a great similarity again, and concluded the works were quite similar---but plagiarism? I couldn't believer it!

When back in my office, I laid the books side by side, and went through several pages, and to my shock the Compton book was virtually a word for word reproduction of Sangster, except for a few minor changes, as if that would cover up his plagiarism. And then, it all came together in my mind. Compton was from Comptonville! I couldn't prove that yet, but at this point, I would have staked my all on that statement. The mystery was solved!

I discovered further as I read his biographical information more closely, that his family was an influential force in a small town in North Carolina, and they had done many things to benefit his hometown, because of that family wealth. I surmised then further that young Compton, before rising to the top of the religious world, had begun to plagiarize William Sangster's writings, and eventually rode them to fame and an influential position in the denomination itself. But in the process he had to eliminate all the memories and all the writings of William Sangster, his family and his work, lest his deceit of plagiarism be discovered, which would have forced him to lose his place and position and future as a leader in the denomination.

No wonder this small town of Comptonville, which was so far off the beaten track, was so uptight about strangers coming to town and asking about William Sangster! The family wealth had built that town, and even the magnificent building of the First Baptist Church there. They probably owned the economy of the town and even the industry, and thus could hire and fire people at will, if they did not go along with this deception and cover up. No wonder there was such a great number of older people and few young people. And who knows how many people even gave their lives, trying to stop the powerful machine in Comptonville, by exposing it in some way.

I could only marvel at God's power, as He truly was the One Who had shown this to us in His own time and providential way. I could hardly wait to tell Dink, and Mac, and William!

But now what was our next step?

13 Can We Take the Next Step?

The next day, as I shared with Dink what I had discovered about Clark Compton and Comptonville and their relationship with the William Sangster matter, he could only say, "Wow, I sure didn't expect dat! Whadda surprise!"

When I asked him what our next move should be in light of these latest findings, he said, "I tink we'd better study da Word an' pray before we does anyting else!"

So we opened our Bibles to Exodus again, to take up the study of Moses, the deliverer of God's people from Egypt. I began by asking if Moses really understood what he was getting into, when he went back to Egypt, committed to deliver God's people from the hand of Pharaoh. He had God's promise that the people would listen, and that Pharaoh would let them go, but we wondered if he really knew how an impossible situation could become even more difficult.

Moses was met by Aaron, as he returned to Egypt, and he told Aaron of the words of the Lord and the signs of God, and how the Lord had convinced him of the call to come and deliver God's people from Egypt! Then Moses and Aaron went and called together the elders of the people of Israel, and they all believed, as did, so it seems, the children of Israel. They all bowed and worshipped! But, again, one wonders if Moses or Aaron or the elders or the people really understood the battle that would ensue, before they were delivered from Egypt? Is it not easy for us to say today as Christians that the battle is the Lord's, and yet fail to understand how fierce the battle could get, and how scarred we may become before God gives the victory?

Take note of Pharaoh's initial response when Moses demanded that he let God's people go. He says boldly, "Who is the Lord that I should obey his voice? I know not the Lord, neither will I let Israel go!" And then he proceeded to make life for the Jewish people even more difficult, by not supplying straw for their work. "Let them gather their straw, and yet do the same amount of work!" was his proclamation. He was determined to lay more work on them, so they would not have time to listen to the vain words of Moses.

And what did the people of Israel do? Go back to tell Moses that they didn't care what Pharaoh did, they were behind him? Not so! They went to Pharaoh to complain, and when he would not bend, they came to Moses to complain and blame him. It is as if they said, "This is your fault, Moses! Why did we ever listen to you?" One wonders what they had expected---a cakewalk down the main streets of Egypt, as they left town with Pharaoh's full blessing?

Then, of course, Moses went and complained to God, asking why He treated these people so badly, and why He had sent him into this kind of a mess. He complained that since God sent him to Pharaoh to speak in His name, Pharaoh had done only evil to God's people, and God had done nothing to deliver this people! Again, one wonders what Moses had expected? No spiritual battle? A meek acquiescence by the monarch of the most powerful nation on earth? Agreement from a spiritually blind potentate who knew nothing and cared nothing about the true God, nor the people of God, nor the will of God, nor the power of God? What was there about this band of Jews as they stood helplessly before Pharaoh, that would scare him one iota, as he laughed in their faces at their ridiculous demands? Nothing---that he could see?

God answered Moses' complaints as He said, "I am the Lord! I have established my covenant to give Israel the land of Palestine! I will bring this people out! I will bring them into the land I have promised them!" Then Moses was told to go tell the children of Israel this, which he did, but still they wouldn't listen to him! Oh, how quickly are God's people discouraged by one growl from the enemy, as they run for the hills for cover? Did they not realize that there can be no victory without the battle? Are we any different today? We run at the first sign of spiritual warfare, wishing to do anything to calm the enemy's fierce wrath against us, as he seeks to close the door of defeat more tightly against our thoughts of doing the will of God.

Then God told Moses to go and speak to Pharaoh once again, but Moses could only complain that if the children of Israel hadn't listened to him, what prospect was there that Pharaoh would hear him---that man of uncircumcised lips?

So, again, God prodded and promised Moses anew, that Pharaoh would do as God commanded, but not willingly. God had to challenge his chosen leader saying, "I have made you a god to Pharaoh! Tell Pharaoh all that I command you---that he must release the children of Israel. It will not be easy, for I will harden his heart, and I will multiply my signs and wonders in Egypt, but Pharaoh will not listen to you at first. You will leave Egypt only because of the judgments that I will send upon Egypt. And the Egyptians will know that I am the Lord, when I stretch out my hand and bring God's people out of Egypt!"

Only after this prompting and reassurance, would Moses and Aaron go back to see Pharaoh. But the point we make in this chapter is that the situation of God's people became even worse than before, in an hour when they probably thought their plight could not possibly deteriorate any further than they had experienced previously.

After a time of prayer, we discussed our own situation. We agreed that the circumstances we faced even now were difficult. Who could predict what we would face, as we faced Clark Compton and this scandal head-on? It was like the old saying, "Cheer up! Things could be worse! So I cheered up, and sure enough, things got worse."

What should we do next in our situation? Do we expect God to solve the problem easily and immediately without battles and scars and moments of apparent defeat? Is not that the attitude of most believers, facing a test or trial in their lives? In our case, what battles will there be? What scars will result? What moments of defeat? What cost before the victory comes---even if it comes in our day?

"Preacha, we'se gots no choice! We can't an' don't need ta go back into Comptonville. We needs ta go straight ta face ole Pharaoh hisself at da seat a' his power! We hast ta go see Clark Compton at da seminary where he's da president! I cain't guarantee it, but dat should be a safe place to challenge da big cat in his own lair, an' at least dat lets him know dat we'se caught him in da very act a' plagiarism---da plagiarism of William Sangster's works."

"Well spoken, my man! But dare we take the next step?" I asked, playing devil's advocate.

"We ain't gots no choice, Preacha! God brought us inta dis, an' God has shown us da further light 'bout Clark Compton! We'se gots ta be obedient ta God, an' do all we can ta right da name of a man of God of years gone by, 'specially, when no one else will or can do anyting!"

14 What Is the Next Step?

As we made preparation to go to the most prestigious seminary of our denomination and confront the president with his sin, I must admit I had some strange sensations about the matter! Was there anyone we could approach first, who would carry the burden for us?

His home church? Well, not the First Baptist Church of Comptonville, though that was not his home church now. And, besides, he still, no doubt, had considerable power there. How about his present church, that is, where his membership now resided?

Or how about taking our case to the board of trustees of the seminary? Would they be open to listen to us? Or would they want to sweep it all under the rug for expediency's sake, and then get rid of us in any way they could? Or would it get tied up in some committee forever, with the result that nothing was ever done about the matter, except the attempt to save the faces of all involved?

And if we did go through the board of trustees, would that only alert Compton of the fact that he had been caught, which would give him a head start to cover his tracks further in any way he could? Could a ruthless man like this be trusted to respond to the matter graciously and confess his sin and step down from his position? I had concluded there was no doubt about his ruthlessness, in light of his years of deceit and cover-up, not to mention the rumors of people who had not survived previous attempts to nail him.

Plus, I had in the past seen enough of denominational politics in good old boy systems, where the glory of God is not supreme, but where expediency rules, whereby many unscriptural things can be justified, including saving our face no matter what the cost! I had discovered in my years in the ministry that there is no more closer knit nor least trustworthy group than a fraternity of clergymen, who are climbing the denominational ladder, as they seek to promote themselves above everything else, including God. This is not to put all of my brothers in the ministry in that category, but it is to note that some are skilled bird dogs, who latch on to the juicy jobs in the churches or in a denomination, with their own advancement the primary sniffing of their souls.

After thinking over this matter awhile, I decided I should at least see if there might be some hope of handling this matter through the seminary board of trustees. I pulled down my denominational annual, which contained the names of all the trustees, and found the name and address of the chairman of the seminary's board. I had to get his phone number through information, but soon I was dialing and waiting to speak with him. His church secretary was kind enough to put me through to him, though I did not give my name.

"Yes, this is Dr. Madison," he greeted me cheerfully.

"Dr. Madison, I understand that you are the chairman of the board of trustees at our largest seminary?"

He answered in the affirmative.

"Could I ask you a question, sir?" I inquired politely.

"Certainly!" was his friendly response.

So far so good, I thought to myself.

"Are you aware of the books of William Sangster, a pastor of our denomination of some years past?" I asked, not wanting to make any accusation immediately against Compton.

"Well, I am aware of the fact that some people just recently have claimed that Sangster authored some books that actually were authored by our seminary president, Dr.

Compton! But the trustees of our seminary have dealt with that and have found no evidence of the truthfulness of such an accusation!" he responded.

"Well, sir, if I may ask another question, have you ever seen any of the Sangster books?" I prodded once again.

It was here that he cut me off, which left me wondering if he was a part of the cover-up or just ignorant of the plagiarism and its cover-up.

"Can I ask to whom I am speaking? You are raising some very serious questions and are even on the border of making them into accusations. Surely, you will have no objection in telling me who you are and why you are calling about this matter?"

"Well, sir, I can understand your concern and desire to know who I am, and, please understand, that under normal circumstances I would divulge that information to you. But I have discovered that anyone who asks questions concerning this matter in Comptonville, Dr. Compton's home town, is ordered out of the city, and is instructed under no uncertain terms to never return to Comptonville again, or else! Are you aware of that?"

I gave him no time to answer but continued, "And are you aware of the elimination and erasure of all evidence in Comptonville that a William Sangster ever lived or even pastored the First Baptist Church of Comptonville from 1900 to 1943?"

He stopped me here, and said rather forcefully, "And there is also a rumor that Elvis Presley is still alive! Look, we have checked this rumor about Sangster thoroughly, and, as I told you before, we found no evidence!"

Then I laid on him the shocker!

"Then you won't mind if I turn my evidence over to one of the leading news agencies of America?"

I purposely did not say "the" leading news agency, for then he would have known it was Turnover News Agency. My answer seemed to silence him for a moment, but then he recovered rather rapidly and replied unmoved.

"I need to go, but I will say this much. We already hired a leading news organization to investigate this matter, and they came back with an exhaustive report that proved there was no credibility to this accusation against Dr. Compton---none whatsoever!"

Quickly, I sought to reply humbly, "But, Dr. Madison, do you not know that money can buy anything, even a false report, if the amount is large enough?"

I was just shooting in the dark on this statement, but if there really was a supposed worthy news organization, which had done an exhaustive report that exonerated Dr. Compton, I had seen enough to know it was a false report!

It was at this point that I heard the phone on the other end go, "click." Dr. Madison had hung up on me! He was either sincerely naïve or deeply involved in the whole scam and scandal. Maybe, it was also proof that Clark Compton was not only unscrupulous in his ways, but also such a smooth operator that he had pulled the wool over the eyes of the entire board of trustees of the seminary. But I had done my duty, and now there was no choice. Dink and I had to go confront Clark Compton!

But what good would that do, I found myself asking? Why would he listen to me, when he hadn't budged an inch before the entire board of trustees of the seminary? I was beginning to sound like Moses, not wanting to face Pharaoh!

There was no way we could not take the next step---wherever it led!

15 Where Will the Next Step Lead?

I had called ahead and made a 10:30 Friday morning appointment with Clark Compton. So after flying into Midwest City early that Friday morning, a rather large city, which housed the seminary, Dink and I were on campus by 10:00. We found his office, and reported to the secretary who we were, and that we had an appointment with the president at 10:30.

I didn't know quite what to expect. Had Dr. Madison warned him to be on the lookout for me? Is that why his secretary gave me an appointment, even when I didn't give my name? Would he be friendly, or would he react immediately, thinking he knew who we were? Or would he give us a "good old boy" smile, and try to woo us to sleep with his spin of the whole situation? I didn't have long to wait to find out, because almost exactly at 10:30 AM, we were invited into his office.

I must admit the office and the position were intimidating! How could a man get this position, and be the man we were accusing him of being? I was about to accost a man, who not only walked in the highest circles of our denomination, but, also, in the world of financiers as well, because of his wealth. He was one of the richest men of our nation. Who was I to walk into his office and confront him? At that moment I had some idea of how Moses felt, when he walked before the throne of Pharaoh to make God's demands upon him. That thought gave me some comfort---I am doing God's business, and the stature of man counts for nothing before Him!

When the secretary told us that Dr. Compton would see us, I grabbed my briefcase, which had a copy of Dr. Compton's so-called book on Psalms, as well as William

Sangster's book on Psalms. As we entered his office, I tried to size him up, and he may have been doing the same with us. He was a man in his early sixties, who was dressed immaculately in a suit and tie, and his friendly, bubbling personality was quite winsome, I had to admit. He insisted that we introduce ourselves, which was easy, as we informed him of our names, and that we were professors at Evanglistic Baptist Seminary in Seminary City. I am sure Dink's manner of speech was challenging to him, since Compton himself spoke such precise and dignified English. But then came the hour of confrontation.

"How can I help you men, today?" he offered, breaking the momentary silence.

I couldn't keep from wondering if he had any suspicions of who we were, having been tipped off by Dr. Madison? Or did he think we were seeking a job at his school? There was no need to delay the inevitable, so I braced myself and began the conversation.

"Dr. Compton, have you ever heard of a William Sangster?" I said abruptly and without apology.

You would have thought I had fired a canon at him, which also indicated he had not talked to Dr. Madison, because at first he seemed to wince, but then he quickly gathered his composure, and without hesitation tried to give a rather nonchalant answer.

"No, I don't think I have. Why do you ask?"

"Well, I ask because your book on Psalms is almost a literal word for word reproduction of William Sangster's work on Psalms, which was written years before yours!" I said, as I pulled the two books from my briefcase.

But I wasn't finished!

"Strange, don't you think, that you haven't heard of him, since he pastored in your hometown from 1900-1943?

And also, Dr. Madison, the chairman of your board of trustees says you would have, since this has come up before, and you were involved in an investigation, which proved there was nothing to the accusation. Are you sure you haven't heard of Dr. Sangster?" I pressed him.

When he seemed speechless, I continued.

"Do you want me to show you the plagiarism in your book of Dr. Sangster's work? And do you know also, that Dr. Sangster's ministry, life and history and existence has been literally eliminated from the history of Comptonville by someone---even from the records of his pastorate there at First Baptist Church for those forty-three years?"

By now he had regained his composure and said softly but firmly, "Gentlemen, I have graciously honored your request for an appointment with me, but not to hear a false accusation repeated against me such as this. I have other more important things to take care of, so please leave my office immediately, before I call the campus police!"

It seemed we were going to get another of those good old police escorts to somewhere, until Dink spoke up.

"Dr. Compton, wouldn't it just be easier ta come clean, an' confess whatcha done, an' ask da Lord's fergiveness as well as da school's?"

At this point, he lost it, and he began to shout at us, which was quite a change from his original demeanor.

"Get out of my office! When I need advice by such as you, a flunky professor at a second-rate seminary [referring to me] and a man who can't even speak the English language [referring to Dink], I will call for you! Get out of my office now and never come back!"

About that time the campus police did come, and escorted us back to our rental car, but it was blocked and we had no where to go.

16 Will Ya Tell Me More about Moses?

I had noticed, as we walked, that Dink had been eyeing one of our escorts or whatever they might be called, as if he knew him. But neither one of them said anything to each other, and I didn't dare ask Dink what was going on. About the time we came to our blocked rental car, one of the walkie-talkies of the campus police sounded, and a few words were spoken. Then we were told to come back, because the president wanted to apologize to us.

I asked, "Do we have a choice?"

One of the policemen indicated no, as he flashed a handgun. I surveyed the campus around us, and saw that it was pretty vacant---a few students here and there. And if we refused to go with them, the police would be given the benefit of the doubt by the students, that they were simply handling a couple of trouble-makers. So why put up a fight here? Dink seemed to agree, as he nodded for me to follow them. So away we went with some concerns, but hoping it didn't show.

We were taken, not to the president's office, but to a remote wooded area on the campus, where we were locked into a room and made to wait a rather long time with no contact from our captors, primarily, Clark Compton. Finally, almost twelve hours later about midnight, the same five goons returned (that's what they were considered to be now). They blindfolded us, tied our hands, and led us to some sort of vehicle. It seemed to me to be a van.

We were driven to an airport, which was about a thirty-minute ride, and then flown for several hours, who knows where or even in what direction. From there we traveled in another van-type vehicle for several hours or more. It was difficult to tell time or distance, not being able to see anything. First, we were on pretty good highway, then on a rough paved road, then on a gravel road, and then on what felt like no road at all. I couldn't begin to guess how long we were on each road, only that the roads deteriorated the further we went, and the slower we traveled according to the terrain. I concluded we must be out in the boonies somewhere---way, way, way, way out in the boonies.

When we stopped the blindfolds were removed, and I could see the sun coming up, which did give me a knowledge of which direction was east, but I had no idea how it could or would do me any good---not when we were this far out in the sticks. They led us to an extremely exquisite cabin, which was well decorated, comfortable, and very inviting as a place of vacation and rest. But who wanted this kind of a vacation? I could see in the kitchen an icebox and a stove as fine as you would find in the best store in town. One of the men told us to be seated, and then he began to speak to us.

"I am sure you men know that you are miles and miles from nowhere! No phone, no television---nothing in the way of communication with the outside world. We will leave you here, and you will have two choices. One, you can stay here and hope someone finds you, but there isn't much hope for that. In fact, during the twenty years we have been working for Dr. Compton, no one has been found in this remote place. But maybe you will be lucky!" he said with a sneer.

"Second, you can try to find your way out, something else no one has ever done. You have plenty of food here, and it will be replenished regularly before it is all gone. So, you can stay here the rest of your lives, or you can try to escape and probably die trying to get out of these mountains. Your choice!"

With those words he and his friends were gone! We were left alone to contemplate our future. Leave and probably die! Or stay and live until we do die! No one will ever know what became of us! Talk about the enemy painting us into a dead-end, no-way-out, never-to-be-seen-again corner---unless the Lord intervened! Brother, this was it---the granddaddy dead-end street of them all!

I asked Dink, "Well, what do you think now?"

He replied with a laugh, "I feels pretty good! We're right where da Lord wants us!"

"By the way," I asked Dink, "who was that guy among the goons that you were eyeing? Did you know him?"

Dink smiled as he replied, "Yeah, I knows him! Dats old Ronnie Filmore, a guy I knew from da gang days! But don't count on him. We never did git along! He hated me an' I never could stand him. I stole his girl friend one time, an' he never did forget it! He challenged me ta a fight one night, an' I beat da tar outta him! He went runnin' off like a little dog wid his tail between his legs! He ain't gonna give us any help. Too much bad blood between us!"

"Well, there went my last hope from the outside world!" I commented. "I thought maybe the way you guys were looking at each other, that he might be a friend and become a help to us."

"Nah, not old Ronnie! But it don't surprise me dat he's turned out ta be a flunky fer some rich guy, doin' da little rich boy's dirty work."

"Well, I do have my briefcase. No one took it from me, although they did search it. I have my Bible, too. Not even a crooked seminary president dared take a man's Bible from him!" I joked.

"Yeah!" Dink echoed. "Tell me more about Moses an' his troubles---an' our great omnipotent God!"

17 Why the Delay for Israel?

Before we had our Bible study, we ate a bite from quite a choice of lunchmeats, fruit, etc. It had been a long time since breakfast! Following this moment of relaxation, if one could really call it that, we reviewed where we were in the life of Moses, and then continued his boxed-in saga.

We had left Moses at the point where the real conflict with Pharaoh was to begin. We had followed him through his rejection to be Israel's deliverer, when he was forty years of age. Then we had gone with him to the backside of the desert, where he spent forty more years of waiting. We even tried to understand something of what must have been going on in his mind, and why he was so reluctant to accept God's call, when he was eighty years old.

Then we had followed him back to Egypt, where he was received by Israel and then rejected again by them. And, understandably, he was forcefully rejected by Pharaoh as well. We could only conclude that at this time he must have had not only second thoughts about this idea of being a deliverer, but also third and fourth and fifth and sixth thoughts about that idea. All he had to hold onto was God's call, God's promises, and God's power, for he had seen no power within himself or the people of God. And it was then, when Moses and the people were at the end of their rope of human hopes, that God began to move, but even then it continued to look hopeless.

The water of Egypt was turned to blood at the command of Moses and the raising of the rod of God. The fish all died, the Nile River stunk to the high heavens, and the Egyptians had no water to drink, as a result of God's judgment. But Pharaoh was unmoved, and went into his palace, until the seven days had passed. No deliverance came! The hopeless situation continued!

The frogs then came upon Egypt as Pharaoh again refused to let God's people go. Frogs in the houses, frogs in the beds, frogs in the ovens, frogs everywhere! Pharaoh called for Moses and asked him to remove the frogs, and he promised he would let God's people go the next day. So Moses removed the frogs, but Pharaoh, when he saw the removal of the frogs, hardened his heart against God again!

Then came the lice, but Pharaoh continued in his refusal to release the people of God.

Then God sent the swarms of flies, even into Pharaoh's house, and his servants' houses, and into every house of the Egyptians. Pharaoh again agreed to let God's people go, and Moses brought the destruction of the flies, but as before, when the flies were gone, Pharaoh hardened his heart further, and would not let God's people go.

Then came the plague on the animals of Egypt, and many of them died, but the Israelites' animals were unaffected. But, again, Pharaoh's heart was only darkened, and he denied Moses' command to let God's people go.

Surely, Moses and the people of God must have wondered at this point where this would all end. Or will it ever end? Will Pharaoh ever relent and do as God commands? Maybe some even began to think it was a stalemate. Maybe Pharaoh was hoping for a stalemate. Maybe some of the Israelites wondered if this was all that God could and would do---just keep afflicting the Egyptians until God would finally give up. Some may have asked, why doesn't God just smite them all, and then we can leave? Why is God so slow in bringing our deliverance? Or some may have said cynically, there is no hope! This is just going to rile up Pharaoh all the more against us, and when he wins he will be more furious than ever before!

And so the battle between God and Pharaoh continued, when hail and fire fell from heaven on the animals, which had remained from the previous plague, but also on every herb, as it seems all the greenery of Egypt was taken away as well. Surprisingly, Pharaoh relented again, as if defeated! He even admitted that he had sinned, and the Lord was righteous, and he and his people were wicked. He would let God's people go! But, again, his heart was hardened and he repudiated his promise!

Then came the plague of locusts all over the land, and Pharaoh again called Moses and told him, "I have sinned against the Lord your God, and you. Therefore, forgive me, I pray, only this once, and ask the Lord your God to take away from me this death." But when the locusts were gone, Pharaoh still would not let God's people go, for God now hardened his heart.

Then came darkness upon Egypt for three days---a darkness so thick that they could not see one another. But the children of Israel had light in their dwellings. Yet, again the Lord hardened Pharaoh's heart, so that he would not let them go.

The lesson for us is that many times, when we are boxed in, we can only wait upon God. The children of Israel could have wondered why it took so long? Why doesn't God just pour out His full power, instead of these smaller judgments, which are only aggravating the enemy? Surely, we should learn also from this experience of the people of God, that our enemy is far more resilient and determined, than we could ever imagine---not that God didn't know this. Pharaoh, who was energized by the great enemy himself, never would give up, it seemed. Satan always dogs us and taunts us, and seeks to trick us and lie to us, and outmaneuver us in our battles with him. About the time we think the battle is over, here he comes against us again, stronger than ever in his determination to fell us.

So we as Christians should not be surprised, when we are assaulted by the enemy, if things seem to get worse and worse, and then even worse, moving from one degree of difficulty to another, until the situation seems to us to be absolutely hopeless. How prone we are in these hours to weep and cry and moan and groan, and even to complain and ask God what He is doing, or why He is not doing more in our behalf.

How many days this battle took place, we are not certain, but those days must have seemed to Moses and his people an eternity---but still there was no hope.

When I indicated I was finished, Dink spoke up.

"Well, Preacha, dat may mean dat we ain't seen nuthin yet of da old enemy's tricks. Makes ya wonder, don't it?"

I stayed awake for about another hour continuing to wonder what would be next for us? I thought of my family, who had no idea where I was! And Dink's family, as well, who were in the same maze of uncertainty. Was anyone looking for us? Not that they would ever find us! Could it be that only the enemy and God knew where we were?

But the Lord gave me peace, for He had brought us through this past day and to this place, when we had no idea what was going on. But the comfort was that His mercy is new every morning, and every evening, and every night, and every second of every hour of every day!

For now, my privilege was to sleep in a comfortable bed, as long as I wanted, with nothing to do tomorrow. I smiled as I thought, I can't do that very often---sleep as long as I want! Always something for which to praise Him.

18 What Do We Do Now?

The next morning, when I finally got up, Dink was no where to be found, nor could I see him anywhere as I looked out the windows. That gave me a little concern for a few moments, until he walked in the back door.

"Looks different in da daytime!" he chirped!

"You sound awfully jolly this morning!" I countered.

"Why not, Preacha? We'se gonna get outta here taday, aint we?"

I laughed and replied, "I'm not worried about getting out of here! It's where we're going after we get out of here that's concerns me!"

"Well, ders a pathway, maybe even da road we took ta get in dis place. I can't find anyting else dat looks like a road but dat! I figures, if we'se jus' follow dat path, it will lead us out sooner or later!"

I didn't mean to sound like the devil's advocate, but I did ask some questions.

"Where is out, when we get there? How long will it take us to get to out, wherever it is? How will we know we are at out, when we get there? Can we make it in one day, or will we have to sleep in the open air somewhere for several nights? What if Compton's men are watching the road when we get to out?" I queried.

Dink laughed, as he knew I was in a way joshing him, and then he replied, "Sure beats sittin' 'round here all day and waitin' ta die, don't it? And den if we doesn't die taday, we will have ta wait till anudder day. Den annuder day! And annuder day! And den annuder day!"

I was concerned he might go on all morning, so I interrupted him, by saying, "As I always say, there's no better day than this day. Or why put off till tomorrow what one can do today! Maybe even dying!"

Dink smiled, as he knew I was kidding. After we both had eaten breakfast, we gathered our few belongings (mine were my precious book by CHM and the Bible in my brief case), and we headed down the beaten path or road or whatever it was. It was the only way in, it seemed, and the only way out. Everything else around us was hideous wilderness through which no man dared to travel.

I had the feeling, as we left, that this seemed too easy! Had there been others who had the same idea? We had been told that no one had ever made it out alive! How did they make it out? The only other way was "dead." As we came to a bend in the path or road, whatever it was, I looked carefully for signs and traces of someone who might be ahead of us, waiting to confront us. But we walked several hours, with no hindrance, except the monstrous wilderness surrounding us. I thought to myself, how do we know where this will take us? Are we walking closer to freedom, or away from it into greater danger?

As we moved along, I wondered if we were in the same remote area of Comptonville, since it sure looked like the same kind of terrain! I surmised that millionaire or billionaire Clark Compton owned this land. It seemed he owned most of Comptonville and the surrounding territory. This was his area to get rid of anyone who might be a threat to expose his plagiarism!

After resting about fifteen, minutes we were off again! I began to wonder where we would be when night came? We rested once again for lunch before continuing our walk. But then it dawned on me at one point that each step guaranteed we would not be able to go back now. We could never reach that comfortable cabin before dark, and that began to be a spooky sensation!

Then following an afternoon break, and several more long hours of walking, it began to get dark! Finally, the sun went down over the mountains, which was a nostalgic moment. It was so beautiful! But then came the realization that it would soon be so dark---pitch dark. I suggested we stop and begin to make preparation to spend the night in the open. But Dink wanted to press on just a little further.

And then it happened! As we set our feet on what we thought was solid ground, it went out from under us, and we went toppling into the heart of the earth---a pit of darkness in which dwelled who knew what! My first thought was, "Is there anything in this deep pit with us?" But who could tell! There could be anything in here from snakes to animals to other human beings---maybe dead ones! As I looked back up out of this pit, I saw the hole was twenty or more feet deep, as there was some light shining upon us from the moon.

Then I thought, "Am I hurt? And what about Dink." About that time, I heard his voice.

"Is you okay, Preacha? Maybe you was right! We shouldda stopped while it was light, cause we sure missed seein' dis here underground jail!"

I thought, that's exactly what this is---an underground jail with a view---a view of the heavens above with bright stars, but no hope of getting out, as far as man could tell. It would have been very easy to panic at this moment! I felt like crying, or flailing my hands in the air, or hitting the side of the pit we were in---anything to relieve the tension.

But then there came a little humor in my mind! Where is Moses when you need him? We're boxed in even worse than before, when we thought such was not possible!

19 Whadda Mighty God We'se Serve?

Understandably, neither one of us slept very well that night. We still weren't certain of what was in the pit with us. It would have been very foolhardy to go crawling around that pit in the dark, using our hands to explore the contents of our forced abode. One might bring back an arm with a stub on the end, or a snakebite on the forearm. Thus there was great apprehension over the contents of the cave, until the sun would rise, and we could see with whom, if anything, we shared our pit of captivity.

Finally, some dim light began to creep into the one end of our dwelling place, and it seemed clear. Then we could see the whole pit, and we gave thanks that it was empty! Next we turned our attention to our bruises and scratches to determine that nothing was broken. Then we tried to piece together some of the branches, which had covered the pit, so we could make a ladder or rope of some kind, but they were all too small. We seemed to be destined to wait upon God. He was our only hope, if we were ever to get out of this place.

Then Dink broke the aura of gloom hanging over us, when he said, "Ya still gots yer Bible, Preacha! Dig it out from dat mess over der, an' tell me da end a Moses an da children of Israel!" And that's what we did, without even checking to see if our food had survived the fall.

I began by noting that we had ended with Pharaoh's latest rejection of God and Moses' command to let God's people go. He had told Moses to get out of his presence, and if he ever saw Moses face again, he would die! Such a statement seemed quite final. Had God failed? Had Moses failed? Had Pharaoh and the great enemy won the battle?

Not so, for God always has the last say in dealing with rebellious men, even though at times He seems to deal with them with great patience. But there comes a time when enough is enough! And God had reached that place with Pharaoh. God will now show His power and wrath in its fearful and shocking fullness!

The last plague was to come at midnight, as the death angel of God would come down over all of Egypt, and every first-born child would die! Can you imagine the number of children of the Egyptians that died that night---all because of Pharaoh's stubbornness? Even Pharaoh's firstborn child was taken from him!

Yet, the blood of a lamb spared the firstborn of each Hebrew family, as that blood was placed upon the doorpost of each home. As the death angel passed through, he would see the blood and he would spare the firstborn of that family, as the blood covered them. No wonder this hour was commemorated for years to follow, and it was called the Passover. The lamb was a Passover Lamb---the picture of Christ to come!

Thus all from the firstborn of Pharaoh to the lowest captive in the dungeon to the first born of the cattle died at midnight that evening. Understandably, there went up a great cry in Egypt at this hour, for there was not a house, where the first born survived---just as God had promised.

It was at this point that Pharaoh and the people of Egypt couldn't get Moses and the children of Israel out of Egypt fast enough. They must go---immediately! Now! Do not tarry! The Egyptians were convinced that if this people did not vacate the land of Egypt immediately, that all of the Egyptians would die---soon! So, make haste! Get out of here! And the Egyptians even gave the Israelites many of their precious possessions to be sure that they would leave the land. Go! Go! Get out of here! Now! Immediately!

God had won the battle! Who had ever doubted and thought He might lose? There were no doubters now! The way was clear for them to leave. This people, who had been boxed in for years, who could see no possibility or way of change, were suddenly on their way by the power of their God, even when it seemed totally impossible for such a thing to come to pass. I can hear some of them saying as they left the land, "I knew God could do it? I knew God would do it! I never doubted God, nor His timing, nor His power, nor His plan!" Doubters suddenly become believers in the reality of victory! They may have even sung a song as they went on their way, like the words which Dink began to recite in his own style---words of praise to our sovereign God.

It is enough to know my sovereign God
is on His throne above;
It is enough to know my sovereign God
rules oer my life in love.

Then we prayed and praised God and committed ourselves and our way to Him, admitting that we didn't know how or when God was going to work, but we trusted Him and His will for us!

The food we had brought from the house was far better than the morning before, as were the aches and pain of our bodies. And why not? The God of Moses was on our side! And if God could get two million people out of Egypt, as they faced the most powerful nation on earth, and He did, He could surely get two men out of a little hole in the ground in His time and in His way, no matter what Clark Compton thought or did, trying to stop Him!

20 Who Is This Visitor?

It was a long day, though our spirits remained high! And when we ate we tried to preserve as much of the food as we could, not because of any unbelief, but we wanted to be good stewards of what God had given us, not knowing what would be next or when and how it would come.

Normally, the night sounds would have been pleasant, sitting on a porch in those mountains, but when you listen to them from a twenty-foot plus pit with no way out, they don't quite have the same effect. After some laughing together and then some prayer, we drifted off to sleep. I found myself saying to God before I was in dreamland, "Okay, Lord! I have learned the lesson of dependence on you alone. Now you can show us Your might and power, and deliver us from this pit. I promise to give You the glory, however the deliverance comes. Please? And thank You for whatever You do for us!" Surely the Lord understood the humorous joy of my heart, as I was confessing my previous unbelief, and stressing my present faith!

Through the night I was aware of rolling over several times on my makeshift bed and pillow. I was more aware of the coldness of the night, than I was the previous night, and also troubled by the hardness of my bed. I longed for the morning and for the warmth of the sunshine. In my drowsiness, I kept wondering why the morning didn't come, and then as I awakened, I began to wonder why it had not come. Finally, with shock I jumped to my feet, as I discovered that someone had covered the opening of the pit above us during the night as we slept.

I awakened Dink, and he too was puzzled! Now we had less light and much more cold and dampness than before, because the sunshine never got to us. But then, all of a sudden, something or someone came tumbling down upon us into the pit. But what or who was it? Was it a bear? Was it a man? Neither Dink nor I could see, because we were covered up by the falling branches.

Then a voice declared, “Hey, you guys! It’s me! Phil Scott! What are you doing here?”

I gave a sigh of relief as I heard that it was Phil, Mac’s reporter, who had been sent into Comptonville to see what he could find out. We had met him in a previous journey. Uncovering ourselves, we hugged one another, and rejoiced over the new addition to our small family of two. We then listened, while Phil told us of his plight in Comptonville.

“Everything went very well, until someone mentioned to me the name of William Sangster. Maybe that person was planted to find out why I had come to town. When I responded to their question, the Gestapo took me blindfolded to a house some distance from Comptonville, and told me I had a choice to live there till I died or try to leave. They told me no one had ever gotten out alive either way, so I could take my pick.”

We told him that was our story, and then Dink noted, “Dats da reason dey covered up da pit, so’s Phil here could fall in it---like we did? And dats der common plan. Ta da house ta be given two choices, an either way, one dies---either in da pit or in da house. Nobody comes back alive!”

“Except us!” I added! “The only thing we don’t know is when or how! I told the Lord last night that I was ready any time! But just think, if we had been delivered sooner, what would have become of Phil! Surely, the Lord’s plan and timing is perfect! Thus we wait upon Him by faith!”

“Yeh, but it also means dey got der eyes on us, an dey knows where we are! But so does da Lord!” Dink added.

21 Will the Victory Ever Come?

We noticed that Phil had done the same thing we did, when we left the house, in that he had taken some food along with him. So we pooled our food supply, ate some breakfast, and then did about the only thing we could do, but the most valuable thing also. We meditated on the Word of God.

We had left Moses and the children of Israel coming forth from Egypt victoriously---literally driven out or thrown out of Egypt, whatever you want to call it. And they were told never to return! So we had seen them leave Egypt with great joy---the place where they had been enslaved for a number of years as a people. What an historic moment this was, if they only realized it!

But their troubles were not over! The Lord spoke to Moses and told him that Pharaoh was going to come after them! God said He would harden Pharaoh's heart, and he and his army would pursue them, but that He would defeat them, so that the Egyptians would know that God is the Lord. Then we are told in the Scripture of Pharaoh's second thoughts, as he said, "Why have we done this, that we have let Israel go from serving us?'

In simple words he states that Egypt has not only lost many children of Egypt, but now he has lost his slave labor as well, and there is no one to do the work, which the children of Israel had done. Or again, in simple words he reasoned, that we can't bring back the thousands and thousands of Egyptian children we lost in death. But we can bring back those slaves. Let's go get them now!

So he got his army ready and took with him six hundred special chosen chariots, plus all the other chariots of Egypt and the captains over them. The Lord's hardening of his heart caused all of this, for God was going to destroy him completely for his part in afflicting His people. Pharaoh overtook this two million or so people. as they were encamped by the sea beside Pi-hahi-roth and before Baal-zephon.

The question at this point is, what will the children of Israel do? By faith will they laugh at Pharaoh as he foolishly pursues them, knowing that God will hit him again and destroy him? Or will they brace themselves, even waiting by faith to see what God will do? Or will they be beside themselves, in light of what they think Pharaoh is going to do to them? They did the latter!

They were in great fear, and they cried out to the Lord, and to Moses, almost blaming him and God for their predicament. The said in this hour, "Weren't there any graves in Egypt, that you have taken us away to die in this desert? Why have you treated us this way, to take us out of Egypt? Didn't we tell you this would happen when we were in Egypt? Didn't we tell you to leave us alone, so we might serve the Egyptians? It sure would have been better for us to serve the Egyptians than for us to die in this wilderness!"

How's that for gratitude to the Lord for His mighty deliverance, and to Moses for coming back to Egypt to be their leader, when he could have kept his peaceful job as a shepherd in the Midian desert area for the rest of his life? What happened to all that rejoicing and supposed faith they had, when they finally saw the victory the Lord gave in Egypt? Oh, how soon we are defeated in our thinking and speech, following a great victory, when we see the enemy raise his head, for a another thrust in his battle against us. It's as if we never had seen the mighty hand of God give victory! We live in the city of defeat, leaving that territory and attitude only for awhile. Yet even as we live there, at the first sign of the enemy, we think its over, and that we're going back to the old place of defeat and enslavement.

Could we really say to our God, "You defeated old scratch once, but You surely cannot or would not do it a second time, so this must be it for us! Woe is us! Get ready for the worst! God is good for only one victory, and then His power is diminished or shelved, as He gives up the battle to the enemy, and forgets His covenant with His people! What a discredit to our God, to look upon Him as a weak, one-victory God, but then to see the enemy as a multi-victory power, who will in some way outlast our God in the battle.

But Moses had the word for them, when he said, "Fear not! Stand still, and see the salvation of the Lord, which He will show to you today, for the Egyptians, whom you have seen today, you shall see them again, no more, forever! The Lord shall fight for you. Just shut up and keep still and watch and see the salvation of the Lord!"

Then Moses stretched forth his hand over the sea, and the Lord caused the sea to divide, so that the children of Israel could walk through the sea that night on dry ground! When the Egyptians got to the sea, they assumed that the waters would remain parted, so they rushed into the midst of the sea, even all of Pharaoh's horses and chariots and men. But the land was no longer dry ground, and the Egyptians got their chariots stuck in the mud at the bottom of the sea! And it is here that God trapped them in the midst of the sea, so they could not get out, even though they had decided that they had better flee the scene.

Then the Lord commanded Moses to stretch forth his hand over the sea once again, and it returned to its normal course, and it drowned all the horses of Pharaoh and his host, till not one of them was left alive. Israel watched as the dead bodies washed up on the seashore. When they saw this great work, they feared the Lord, and believed the Lord and his servant Moses.

When I stopped to ask what lessons we could learn from this, Dink spoke with some conviction.

"Boy, God's people, includin' me---we sure is fickle, ain't we? We never seems ta want ta give God da benefit of da doubt, nor da credit fer nuthin. We always expects Him ta either never send a trial or test, or ta get rid of it, immediately! An' even when He gives da victory, we are still gloomy people wid sour faces an' attitudes, spectin' da worst even in da face of a little setback. Our idea always seems ta be, Poor God! He can't do nothin' right ta please us! He shoulda never let da trial or test come in da first place! Or He shoulda let it only stay fer a little while! He shouda bailed us out sooner dan He did! And He can only give us one trial a year or even durin' our lifetime, cause dats all He's good fer, we tink!"

We discussed how this applied to our small trial---small compared to trials so many other believers had faced. Judson, who spent eighteen months in a filthy windowless prison in the worst heat imaginable. Carey, who had a wife who went insane on the mission field. Brainerd, who faced the most defying wilderness, far more hideous than our wilderness, and he faced it in the most severe winter weather, while our days and nights were nothing compared to his. What had we ever faced, even now, in comparison to our Lord's agony on the cross?

The remainder of the day passed as slowly as the previous ones. But at least our spirits were high, as our faith in our great God had soared from the study of His Word. Tomorrow is in His hands!

22 Is This the Beginning of Victory?

I was rejoicing that night, when I drifted off to sleep, and I really slept soundly for the first night since leaving home. No tossing and turning, no being awake for an hour or two. Maybe I was getting used to the hard bed and pillow and even the cold at night. So it was easy to sleep later in the morning, partly because there was nothing to do when we woke up any way.

It wasn't until the sun began invading our little abode, that I began to stir a bit, but when I finally opened my eyes, I got the shock of my life. There standing at the top of the pit, was a man looking down on us! It was difficult to distinguish who he was, since he was standing between us and the light. All I could see was a man in overalls, with a gun (rifle or shotgun) cradled in his arms, which wasn't very encouraging.

Then he spoke in a rather gruff-sounding voice! "Come on men, it's time to get out of here. We're burnin' daylight!" He then threw a rope to us, and one by one he pulled us up, including my briefcase with my books. I wasn't going to leave them there, though I would gladly part with everything else in that pit! My first inclination was to ask him who he was, but he seemed to be a man of few words (which was to be expected if he lived in these mountains by himself). So I just shut up and did as I was told, as did the others. We gladly accepted his helping hand to get us out of the pit, even though we didn't know what might come next.

When we were all out of the pit, he grabbed the rope, rolled it up, and said, "Come on! Follow me, but be quick about it! We could have visitors at any time!" I thought to myself, "Gladly!"

We must have walked a number of hours, even in places where there was no road or pathway. I was so delighted to be free from that pit, that I hadn't noticed the time of our deliverance, to use a good Biblical word. Finally, we came to a truck that I assumed was his. He informed us that we all would have to ride in the back of the truck covered up, lest someone see us and know of our escape. So we all crawled in and pulled what covers he had over us. I must admit that I cheated a little, and kept a small peephole for myself, out the back of the truck. We took off through the wilderness over slow and bumpy terrain, where there seemed again to be no road. I wondered how he had ever found this place, unless he was one of Compton's men---not a very pleasant thought!

We rode for about an hour and never saw a real road. We just wound around the mountain, taking whatever the mountain would give us in way of a passage. Finally, we pulled up in the front of a small house built in the side of the mountain. He invited us to come in, then served us food without saying one word. I sized him up as being about sixty plus or so years old, but in good health, as he moved around without showing any aches or pains of aging. Finally, he sat down with us and asked, "Which one of you is Pointer---Ira Pointer?"

I wondered how he knew of our plight, and even my name, but I nodded that I was his man, and I didn't ask him any other questions. I waited to see his next move.

"Well, I told you that when you needed me, I would be there for you! Remember?"

So, he was the mysterious man on the phone! But that still didn't tell me who he was, or why he had helped us!

Then he briskly ordered us, "Follow me! I have something I want to show you!"

He took us to a room built back into the mountain. Evidently, it was a secret room, which we entered through a closet with a hidden door. The room was filled with bookshelves, and they were also filled with what I took to be his library. He walked over to one of the shelves and told us to follow him, and then he ordered each one of us to take one of the books from the shelf.

We followed his command. He was doing something, but I couldn't figure out what!

"Look at the title page!" he barked again.

Then he pointed to each one of us separately, and instructed us to give him the title of the book, which we had in our hands, and the name of the author.

"*A Commentary on Genesis* by William Sangster!" I replied, with some surprise.

"*A Commentary on Luke* by William Sangster!" Dink answered.

"*A Commentary on Romans* by William Sangster!" Phil echoed.

"I've got them all men! All the books and articles that Pastor Sangster ever wrote! Come on back into the living room, where it's more comfortable. I know you are tired, but let me tell you all about William Sangster and his books and the city of Comptonville! That's what got you all into this mess, wasn't it?"

Then he turned to Phil, and asked, "Are you the guy from the news agency?"

Phil nodded in the affirmative.

"And you must be the famous Dink, the former mafia and gang member, who was converted to Christ a few years ago?" he said, looking at Dink.

23 Can I Tell You My Story?

I noted that our host had gone from being a quiet man to being quite a talker with more knowledge than we could have imagined. He had the floor, and though I wanted to ask him some questions, we just listened. Maybe he would tell us what was on his mind, and then we could quiz him, if necessary. But I had to admit, that it was with eagerness that we awaited his story.

"My name is George Carlson. I was born in the same month and year in Comptonville as your friend, Clark Compton. He was born on the right side of the tracks, and I was born on the other side of the tracks, as the saying goes, to the poorest of the poor. We grew up together, went to school together, competed against each other, and I guess if he ever had a friend, I was it, though it was a strange friendship. For you see, the competition for things was not quite fair. Old Clark was a spoiled rich boy, who always had to have his own way, because his father coddled him and spoiled him, as did the whole community, in order to stay in the good graces of his daddy.

"As a result, he played quarterback on the football team, even though I could run faster, cut through tacklers better, and throw the ball twice as far as he could. As a football player, he stunk up the stadium, every Friday evening. No one dared say a word, because his daddy controlled everything. With one word, Daddy Compton could have wiped out Comptonville, or any one in Comptonville, who gave him or his son trouble.

"He and I, though we had something of a friendship on the surface, never liked each other. I was one of the only ones who would ever stand up to little Clarkie, and I especially enjoyed getting him in my sights on the football field during practice, when I played defense and he played quarterback. He never did forget the day that I cold-cocked him. He was unconscious for several hours. They even had to call an ambulance! My plea was that it was just part of the game, but he never believed me!

"My daddy was a deacon in the church and was about the age of his father, who was a deacon, also. And you can guess who ran the church. The only man I ever knew, who would stand up to him, was Pastor Sangster. He didn't care if it did blow the town sky high. He told Mr. Compton many times to back off of something, because it was not Biblical. And Mr. Compton didn't like it and he threatened, as always, to pull his money out of the church, and even Comptonville. But he always backed off. Pastor Sangster didn't care! He was bound by the Word of God!

"Well, anyway, to get on to the heart of my story, Pastor Sangster wrote numerous manuscripts for books, mostly commentaries, and he would mail them, so he thought, to the publishers. But Mr. Compton controlled the post office as well, so there was a suspicion in my daddy's mind that the publishers never saw those manuscripts, because they were confiscated by the Comptons. If they were mailed, my daddy surmised that any favorable letter from the publishers was also intercepted by the Comptons.

"Thus they controlled without his knowledge all of Dr. Sangster's mail. He never did get any of his books published, except for a few that he published on his own, with the help of Mr. Compton. I'm convinced that any advertising which Dr. Sangster sent out on these, was confiscated as well at the post office. Thus no orders ever came in for Dr. Sangster's books. Only a few were ever sold---to Dr. Sangster's friends and family. Pastor Sangster eventually died never knowing the truth of the greatness of his books. And when old man Compton finally died, guess who got the copies of all those books? You guessed it---Clark Compton! And no one knew the difference, except my daddy!

"He may not have had a great education, and he may have been just a common laborer, but he was a voracious reader and a keen student of the Bible. He read, probably, as many commentaries as most preachers read, and he was a crackerjack of a Bible teacher. He said Dr. Sangster's books were on the quality of the best commentaries he had ever read. So, he carefully collected them, one or maybe even two copies each of the books, and he told no one of his sacred commitment to someday see that they were presented to the church at large in the author's name.

"But the sad part is that he died, never able to keep that commitment, because of the power of the Comptons. But I have taken these books as a sacred trust, and by the grace of God, I won't die till I have kept that commitment! And if in the process, Clark Compton is exposed for his plagiarism and treachery, so be it, but that is not my primary goal. My primary goal is to get these books published in Dr. Sangster's name!"

I noticed a few tears in his eyes, as he mentioned this commitment, and the fact was evident, that this common laborer with the seemingly external leather attitude, possessed a very tender heart. Then he continued.

"In the passing of the years young Compton went to college to study for the ministry. I think he thought it would be an easy way to make a name for himself, rather than having to work with and for his daddy! But he was a flop as a student and as a preacher, but his daddy's pocketbook saved him again. A large donor can influence a lot of things in some places!

"Finally, he finished all his degrees, even a doctorate, but again, not all the credit could go to him. He wanted to teach in a college or seminary, but no one would hire him. Finally, a small college about a hundred miles north of here hired him to teach the Bible. Unknown to anyone, he took the commentaries of Pastor Sangster, and he began to teach the material from them in his classes. I know, because that is where my son went to college, and he had one of his classes, and when he shared Compton's notes with me, I compared them with one of these Sangster books, and sure enough, it was not Compton's material, but Sangster's.

"But by teaching Dr. Sangster's material, he became the rage of the campus! What insight! What scholarship! You must publish this material, he was told! So he did! He published Sangster's works under his name, and they became some of the best commentaries of the day, and are still the favorites of many of God's people. But during the early days, as he began to publish Sangster's works, he also conducted a search and destroy mission for any of the original Sangster books, which had been printed earlier under the author's name, and which had slipped through his daddy's net of confinement. He did it to protect himself!

"But to get back to the saga of Clark Compton. It wasn't long until a seminary was calling upon him to teach, and again, he was heralded as a great scholar and teacher. I don't know how he kept up the charade, as he moved into the highest levels of scholarship, but he did. I guess it was two things. First, his fake winsome personality and charisma, as he had become, no longer the brat he was as a kid, but smooth Mr. Personality and Mr. Nice Guy. Second, couple that with the writings of Dr. Sangster, and he had hit the big time, as far as acceptance and seeming success. This was the first time in his life that he was accepted and not considered the community brat!

"If any questions did arise about plagiarism, they were deflected either by firm denial or by elimination of that person somehow, if it was a serious or dangerous threat. His family already owned that five thousand acres of land in the mountains, so he just set up a house, which became a death house, but which also had a path to the pit, which became a way of death also. Only the Lord knows how many people left this world by that means, and how many bodies are buried in those mountains, where they will never be found, just because they raised questions about his books. And no one can prove anything against him.

"I had searched for that death house for years, but I had to be careful, lest his flunkies saw me, and I ended up in that same place. I found the house just a few months ago, as well as the death pit, but I have never been able to find any graves---he has been that slick."

I didn't know about the others with me, but I gave a sigh of relief, as I understood God's providence was involved in his finding the death house and the pit, just before we landed there! How close we came to becoming the latest victims, if what George was telling us was true.

He then promised he would answer any questions we might have, after we took a brief break. As he went outside, we all looked at each other in a quiet amazement!

Dink spoke up first, when he said, "If I hadn't a gone through dis myself, I never woulda believed sucha story! Blatant plagiarism! A death house! A death pit! All in da name a Jesus an da teachin' of da Bible! Jesus sure was right when He said, 'Beware a men dat comes in da clothin' of sheeps, but inwardly, deys ravening wolves!' We sure got ourselves a hold of a wolf, didn't we!"

24 Dare We Challenge Him?

When we began again, after our break, I had the first question.

"How many people from the town do you think stood up to the Compton family over the years concerning this matter and went the route of the death house or pit?"

"I can't be sure," he answered. "But there were some mysterious disappearances from Comptonville, which were never solved, and you know that the Comptons had the police in their back pocket! Plus there were others in town, who just left to get out from under the pressure of being under suspicion and not knowing what might happen to them, if they began to ask questions. Plus the deck was stacked, as far as not only the city officials, but also some state officials with the Comptons' contacts and influence. There may have been some good men in the state political offices, but the Comptons were such a respected and powerful family, no one would believe any accusations against them! Money and power talk, especially against common people of little or no means!"

Dink asked the next question.

"Has his boys been loyal ta him over da years? Dats an awful long time fer his henchmen, who is doin' da dirty work, ta stay loyal!"

I thought that sounded like a Dink question. He looked at things from the criminal's view, thinking maybe he might learn something.

"Well, there has been a turnover through the years. That's a lot of years, so there was bound to be some turnover. Like so many things, we never knew the inner workings of the Compton family, as far as their help. We never knew if those men left voluntarily or were forced out for lack of loyalty, or what!"

I guess we were tired, and our minds were ready to rest, so I thought I would end it on a joyful note, when I declared, "Well, I guess we've got Clark Compton now. We have the evidence, and we can count on him being in jail soon for his crimes!"

George smiled, and then laid the blockbuster on at least me, when he said, "If I was a betting man, I wouldn't lay money on it!"

"Do you mean with the Sangster books themselves, we don't have enough evidence to nail him? Plus, the death house, the pit, and on and on I could go? That's not enough evidence?" I asked in amazement.

"Son, as the saying goes, you ain't see nothin' yet! I've seen Clark Compton at work for years. He's a liar, yes, and a plagiarist, and behind some murders. But he is also smooth and persuasive and connected with the most powerful agencies and men of the nation! And he is an expert in conning anyone and everyone, if necessary, especially juries, if he ever goes to a jury trial. He can make the most innocent man, who would raise his voice against him, look guilty, while he the guilty man is seen as innocent. Let me warn you, that he's like a wild animal, when cornered, but he's also as smart as a whip in the area of judicial warfare, and he has the best of lawyers which money can buy. Do you want to go up against that? I guarantee that the next level of your warfare with him will be worse than this little skirmish you have just come through. This thing is a long way from being over! Mark my word, and go to the bank on it!"

I must admit that my joy and enthusiasm took a little hike with that speech! I could tell it was the same with the others! And just when we thought we were a few days from seeing him in jail! Dare we challenge him?

I was, however, greatly encouraged, when Dink chimed in, "Sounds like annuder job fer our great omnipotent God! Why not? He certainly has more power dan a little two-bit, tinhorn, puffed up, con man! Thus da question is not, who is Clark Compton or who is God! Dats clear. But da question is, does we trust our great God?"

I thanked Dink for the challenge, but I felt I needed to get up off of the floor spiritually, as George had decked me, and properly so! I suggested we study the Word, but our host said we had to get out of his house as soon as possible, lest we be discovered there. With that I agreed, for it would be better to let them think for awhile that we were dead, than to catch us escaping. I also wondered if they would be checking the house and the pit any time soon. That was another reason to get out of this territory immediately.

George told us that not only were we leaving his house, but so were the books. He figured, if we had them, there was no way that Compton could get his hands on them and destroy them. So we all began to box up the books, but it took longer than anticipated, as we stopped to look them over as we handled them. Finally, they were ready to go, and so were we! I wondered how we would be able to get in the truck, but we did, and we were off! I didn't know where we were going, but the first concern was just to get out of the Comptonville territory---and be quick about it!

Then we would be ready to face the battle for the recognition of a great man of God, whose life and reputation and writings had been pirated by a scoundrel of a father and a son!

25 Can We Trust Him?

After traveling about thirty minutes, we were back on a normal road---no more mountain roads. But then, almost immediately, we heard a siren whining behind us, and my heart fell, like it had when I dropped into the pit! I thought, "Oh, no, not again!" I must admit, I wondered what the Lord was doing now, as it had to be the Comptonville police or someone who knew Clark Compton, and had been alerted to be on the lookout for us!

We decided it would be best to stay hidden, and let George see if he could get us out of this on his own. What could we do to help anyway, except let the officer know we were hidden in the truck bed?

I heard George speak to the officer.

"Hey, Sam! What can I do for you today?"

"Oh, I just saw you driving by and wanted to ask if you had seen any strangers out your way or around this area anywhere!" Sam replied.

"Do you think I would help them, if I had?" George replied, not lying, but just asking a question.

"What ya got in the truck bed there?" the officer asked again.

"Oh, just the guys you're lookin' for! All of them!" George shockingly replied.

Then the conversation got very serious!

"George, can I tell you something in confidence?" Sam asked.

"Why me?" George countered.

"Well, because I know you don't go along or get along with Clark Compton!" Sam said unexpectedly.

"I think you're planning something to help bring him down!" he continued. "And if you are and need help, I want you to know that you can count on me!" Sam blurted out in a softer voice that I could hardly hear. "That's one reason I'm not going to inspect your truck! I think you do have those men under those coverings, but I want to help you. I'm tired of working for the Comptons and want out, but you're the only man I can trust around Comptonville!"

"How do I know I can trust you, if I was planning something?" George asked. "You could be a plant by Clark Compton to get to me and find out if there is something going on!" George countered.

"I knew it would be hard to convince you, but one of these days there will come a show down, and I will stand with you! I guarantee it! Now, have a good day and take care of those boys in your truck bed and whatever else you have in there! I'll fill out a report that I saw you, but I saw nothing in your truck, but I won't' say I didn't look!"

With that we were back on the road and on our way out of Comptonville territory. I couldn't wait to talk to George about Sam---if he thought he was on the level.

It took us about three hours to get to a larger metropolitan area, and we heard nothing more from any police officials along the way. We called our families, who understandably were elated to hear from us. There we also rented a truck to haul the Sangster books back to Seminary City. We finally told George goodbye, but not before we asked him about Sam.

"Well," he said thoughtfully, "time will tell. I've known him for years, and he's been a good friend, even though he worked for the Comptons. I kind of think he's on the level, but we'll wait for him to make the next move! Let him prove himself in some crucial situation, whenever that might be. Don't be in too big of a hurry to trust anyone has been my rule through all these years!"

26 How Can We Fail with God?

When we left George, we rented a car. Since we were going to drive most of the night to get to Seminary City, I asked one of the other men to drive, so I could give them some spiritual food to think about, while we traveled during the daylight hours which remained. Dink agreed, and as he drove, I read to them some choice thoughts from CHM on the chapters in Exodus, which we had just covered.

> God's counsel shall stand, and He will do all His pleasure. The enemy may oppose, but God will ever prove Himself to be above him; and all we need is a spirit of simple, childlike confidence and repose in the divine purpose. Unbelief will rather look at the enemy's efforts to countervail than at God's power to accomplish. It is on the latter that faith fixes its eye. Thus, it [faith] obtains victory and obtains abiding peace....It [faith] rests not on the ever-shifting sands of human affairs and earthly influences, but upon the immovable rock of God's eternal Word. That is faith's holy and solid resting-place. Come what may, faith abides in that sanctuary of strength. (Mackintosh, *Notes on the Pentateuch: Genesis to Deuteronomy*, p. 149)

Dink kept saying "Wow!" all the way through the reading of this quote. Then he commented, "Dat sounds like it was written just fer us! Da enemy opposes, but God proves Himself---all we needs is ta trust Him, rather dan looking at da enemy's power, or trustin' in da sinking sands a man an' earthly tings. Wow! Read us annuder one!"

> The wildest mistake a man can possibly fall into is to act without taking God into account. Sooner or later, the thought of God will force itself upon him, and then comes the awful crash of all his schemes and calculations. At best, everything that is undertaken independently of God, can last but for the present time....What a sad mistake, therefore for a feeble mortal to set himself up against the eternal God... Eternal confusion shall be inscribed upon all the opposition of men and devils. This gives sweet rest to the heart in the midst of a scene where all is apparently so contrary to God and so contrary to faith. Were it not for the settled assurance that "the wrath of man shall praise" the Lord, the spirit would often be cast down while contemplating the circumstances and influences which surround one in the world. (Mackintosh, p. 141)

Dink responded again, by saying, "I sees what's ya mean, Preacha, when ya says ya needs ta stop after ever sentence of dat guy CHM. Boy, accordin ta him, da enemy ain't got no chance against da Lord---an' he's right! Makes me feel sorry fer poor old Clark Compton! He sure acted widout takin' God inta account! An it's sure gonna catch up wid him! I'd hate ta be in his sneakers taday!"

Phil spoke up and kidded Dink about not being able to get a word in edgewise, so I told Phil that this one was his!

> Thank God, "we look not at the things which are seen, but at the things which are not seen; for the things which are seen are temporal; but the things which are not seen are eternal." (2 Cor. iv. 18.) ....How fully might the truth of this be seen in the case of both the oppressed and the oppressor, as set before us in our

chapter! Had Israel "looked at the things that are seen," what were they? Pharaoh's wrath, stern taskmasters, afflictive burdens, rigorous service, hard bondage, mortar and brick. But, then, "the things which are not seen," what were they? God's eternal purpose, His unfailing promise, the approaching dawn of a day of salvation, the burning lamp of Jehovah's deliverance. Wondrous contrast. Faith alone could enter into it. (Mackintosh, p. 141)

Phil could hardly wait now to respond.

"How easy to look at that which we can see, and totally miss the eternal---that which we cannot see. Is not the eternal by far the most important to the Christian! How can the believer fail, if his eye is fixed upon God's eternal purpose. But without faith he will stumble all over the place, discouraged by what he sees through the fleshly eye! I agree with Dink! Poor old Clark Compton hasn't got a chance, but that doesn't mean it will be easy. It means whatever he pulls on us as God's people, he cannot win. However dreary it may look to us in the coming battle, he cannot win! God has already won the battle. May we never forget that!"

We couldn't help but sing,

Faith mighty faith, the promise sees,
 And looks to God alone.
Laughs at impossibilities
 And cries it shall be done.
And cries it shall, it shall be done,
And cries it shall, it shall be done.
Laughs at impossibilities
And cries it shall be done!

27 Could the Sacred Trust Be Ours?

When we finally arrived in Seminary City, we decided we had better store the books in a secure place. So we found a storage unit and rented it and unloaded our precious cargo. We agreed we would bring the other Sangster books to this place, the ones we had found, so that all the books would be together in this one secure place. We locked our unit securely (we bought the biggest lock that the storage unit sold). Trusting the books were safe, and with the promise we would keep in touch with one another, we went our separate ways.

Several days went by without my hearing from anyone, and I was glad, as I was recovering from the ordeal of the pit and the other accompanying circumstances. I was surprised how worn out I really was, but decided it must have been not only the physical exhaustion, but also the mental fatigue as well. It was on the third day home that I finally heard from Dink.

“Preacha, has ya heard from Mac? He said he couldn’t get ya, so he called me an’ asked me ta tell ya da latest! Old George sure was right, Preacha, cause Clark Compton has boxed Mac in at Turnover News Agency now! He’s fixed it so Mac’s liable ta lose control of TNA ta keep Mac from exposing ole Clark!”

“But how could he do that?” I asked in unbelief.

“Sneaky Clark, dug up da fact dat TNA was owned by Mac an’ his two brothers!” Dink explained. “Each one of dem has 25% of da stock, an’ Mac has 50% of da stock, which made Mac da major shareholder. So it was always a stand off, an’ da brothers just let Mac run da ting, since it was makin’ dem money. Dey aren’t Christians, an’ dats what deys interested in anyhow---makin’ money!

"Well, Clark has offered da brothers five times da value of der stock, an da brothers are gonna sell der stock ta him, which will make Clark Compton an equal partner wid Mac in TNA. Mac figures when dat deal is done, den old Clark will oppose ever ting he has been doing, just so he can kill TNA, and silence Mac. Even ifs he can tie Mac up in court over da matter of who leads TNA, he can keep Mac from doin' what he wants ta do, 'specially exposin' him, an' probably even bankruptin' Mac in da process!"

"I guess Mac is worried!" I declared.

"Well, he was, till Phil shared wid him whats we'se been studyin' in Exodus, an' now Mac has put it all in da hands of da Lord!" Dink explained with rejoicing. "He sees it like us---Clark can kick up his heels all he wants, but God will have da last word, somehow!"

"But dat ain't all!" Dink continued. "George is missin'. He disappeared just afters he let us off, an he ain't been seen since. Seems Mac has some contact in Comptonville, but I don'ts know who, but deys keepin' an eye on tings der! Mac figures George has either been taken captive by Clark's goons, or he's gone ta da hills on his own ta keep from gettin' captured by dose guys. Either ways nobodys seen him since he let us off."

I thought as I got off the phone, there's no need to worry about George, if he took to the hills. He could live out there for the rest of his life without detection or capture!

But then again, he could be dead or dying, even in the pit! Who then would inherit the sacred trust of the Sangster books?

28 What Do You Do with Leaky Vessels?

Dink came by later in the day at school and said he had been reading Chapter 15 of Exodus. He said he was struck by the fickleness of the faith of the children of Israel, right after seeing God's mighty power in the Exodus and in the destruction of Pharaoh and his army. His observation, included, that they were leaky vessels! But then in some ways, aren't we all. But were we that bad?

I opened my Bible, and we noted the great joy and exultation of their hearts, just after the destruction of their enemies in the Red Sea. I read the main verses from Exodus 15:1-2:

I will sing unto the Lord
    for He has triumphed gloriously!
The horse and his rider
    He has thrown into the sea!
The Lord is my strength and song,
    and He is become my salvation!
He is my God
    and I will prepare Him a habitation.
He is my father's God---and I will exalt Him!

Then Exodus tells us of the death of Pharaoh and his army in the sea (verses 3-10), but then it continues exalting the Lord in verses 11-12:

Who is like unto Thee, O Lord, among the gods?
Who is like Thee?
    glorious in holiness!
    fearful in praises!
    doing wonders!

Thou in mercy hast led forth the people
whom Thou hast redeemed!
Thou hast guided them by thy strength
unto Thy holy habitation!

But, oh, how soon they complain and evidence the lack or loss of their faith, which should have been so strong at this point of their lives. Note the following evidence of their leaky vessels, when it came to maintaining a steady and constant faith:

1. At Marah, when there was no water, the people murmured against Moses, asking, What shall we drink? And so Moses cried unto the Lord, and the Lord showed him a tree, which he cast into the bitter waters, and they became sweet! (see Exodus 15)

2. When in the Wilderness of Sin, and they had no food, the whole congregation murmured against Moses and Aaron, and faithlessly said, "Would to God we had died by the hand of the Lord in Egypt, where we sat by the fleshpots and ate bread to the full! Moses, you have brought us forth into this wilderness to kill this whole assembly with hunger!" And it was here that the Lord gave them manna to eat. (see Exodus 16)

3. At Rephidim, when there was no water once again, the people said, "Give us water that we may drink!" Moses replied that they were tempting the Lord by their attitude. The people said again to Moses, "Why did you bring us up out of Egypt, to kill us and our children and our cattle with thirst?" But God through Moses gave them water from the rock! (see Exodus 17)

Oh, how fickle the human heart! On the mountaintop top one day and in the valley the next! Praising God and His servant one day and murmuring against both the next! Satisfied one day, but dissatisfied the next! Full of faith one day, but bankrupt the next! Sweet and happy one day, but bitter and complaining the next! Loving God one day, but doubting God the next! Hopeful one day, but hopeless the next! Happy one day, but down in the dumps the next!

Should not a true faith be more steady and level, rather than on a roller coaster ride from one day to the next? Should not a true faith temper and moderate one's emotions, rather than allow the circumstances to whip the emotions all over the lot? What good is a faith, which rides the waves of the circumstances around us, being up if circumstances are acceptable to us, and down when the circumstances are in the pits? Mackintosh says again:

> Its (faith's) eagle gaze can pierce the gloomy clouds which gather around the tomb, and behold the God of resurrection displaying the results of His everlasting counsels, in the midst of a sphere which no arrow of death can reach. It (faith) can take its stand upon the top of the Rock of Ages, and listen, in holy triumph, while the surges of death are lashing its base. (Mackintosh, p. 143)

I added, that the strength of faith is not within us, but its strength is the ground of its focus---the greatness and power of God.

About then the phone rang! It was the president of our seminary, Dr. Graham. He spoke with concern saying, "Dr. Pointer, I have all the confidence in the world in you and Dink! But I need some answers. Can I see you today?"

29 Who's on Our Side?

When I shared the content of the phone call with Dink, he concluded that Clark Compton was putting pressure on Dr. Graham to deal with us in some way, in light of our claimed interference in his life. I was glad for the confidence that Dr. Graham had in us, in light of my having proved myself in a previous situation. (Belcher, *A Journey in God's Glory*)

I told Dink we were supposed to see Dr. Graham in half an hour in his office. I wondered what exactly the accusation would be, and what kind of evidence Compton would hatch up against us! I could only imagine what charges we would face, when I remembered that no one was in the room with us, when we visited Compton, except him. Never mind what he had done following our visit to his office to try to eliminate us completely!

I told Dink I would meet him in the president's office in thirty minutes, and that I had to do something first. I left to take care of that matter, and was back in the office in plenty of time, carrying my briefcase with some very convicting evidence against Clark Compton. Thus it was with a fairly solid confidence that we entered the president's office and sat down with eager hearts to hear the accusations.

Dr. Graham smiled, as he noted, "I guess this is a result of men standing for the truth! But, also, it is the result of other men not standing for the truth! Some how I would like to warn your accuser of the results of dealing falsely with us in any matter, since I have been through this before with you and previous accusers."

I smiled, and asked him what the accusations were this time.

He replied, "You have been accused of threatening a seminary president in his office; of disturbing the peace in a public library in another state; of doing the same in a Baptist church in the same state and city; of kidnapping a man who lives outside that city; of trashing a home in the mountains, as you stayed there one night; and of stealing valuable documents from the home of the man you kidnapped! I have it all in the police reports from the several different places where you have been accused. But, the man who brings the charges says he is a fair and kind soul, who doesn't want to prosecute you, and if you will resign your positions here at our school, and return his valuable documents, and stop your harassment of him and his life, school, and hometown, he will drop all the charges!"

"The man bringing the charges is Clark Compton, and all his accusations are false, and I can prove it, and give you his motive for all these ridiculous charges right now!" I declared, as I reached into my brief case and brought out two books.

I showed him the first book, and he acknowledged that he had seen it, and that he knew the author well, and that he had even read some of his books, and that he was our accuser. I then replied, "But he is not the author of that or any of the other books which bear his name!"

I handed him the second book, the one authored by William Sangster, and then asked him to compare the books and their publication dates, and then tell me that Clark Compton wrote the book which bears his name.

Dr. Graham flipped through the two books, and then began comparing them page by page. Finally, with surprise he looked up at me, and shaking his head he said, "I can't believe it? Compton plagiarized Sangster's book?"

"Not book, but books!" I informed him. "Every book that Clark Compton has written is the result of plagiarism. They all are the works of William Sangster, a man who pastored in his hometown for forty-three years. The rest of the story is rather long, but that is the basic truth of the matter, and the reason Compton is after us with all those false accusations. In fact, it may sound far-fetched, but he would kill us if he could! In fact, he tried! The knowledge and proof, which we have, will destroy his life and ministry! He thinks he has to get us with his lies and henchmen before we get him with the truth!"

Dr. Graham sat there dumbfounded with his mouth wide open and a look of amazement on his face!

"Let me say to both of you, I would not believe these accusations from anyone else but you two men. I know your integrity---it is unshakeable! What can I do to help you in this battle, which you are facing?"

I went ahead and filled him in on the whole story from the beginning to the end. I told him what had really happened at the library, at the church, at Compton's office, at the death house in the woods, in the pit, at George Carlson's home, and then our escape from it all. We then left his office, knowing we had an ally---someone who would be on our side, when the fireworks began.

As we went back to my office, Dink pontificated on a section he had read in CHM.

"I remembers him sayin' dat der are two tings dat da servant of da livin' God should not regard---neither da fear of man nor da favor of man! Neither of dese matters ta da man of God, who holds a divine commission an' enjoys da divine presence!" (Mackintosh, p. 145)

Then he added, "But it sure is nice ta have somebody on our side fer a change---besides da Lord!"

30 Are We under Arrest?

I stayed later that day seeking to come to grips with what we faced, and by the time I left my office it was dark. My walk to my parked car seemed rather normal, until I actually got to the parking lot. It was there that what seemed to be no more than a parked van came alive with men in hoods, as the doors of the van opened, and they grabbed me and stuffed me into their vehicle. Quickly the doors slammed shut, and the van drove off slowly, as not to create any disturbance. Immediately upon seizure my head was covered by a hood with no eyeholes. I thought, here we go again---Compton's goons!

Soon we stopped and waited for fifteen to twenty minutes, and I heard the doors open again, and there was another struggle, as they were grabbing someone else in the manner they had taken me. I heard a familiar voice speaking to his captors until it was hushed, and there was no doubt that they had grabbed Dink as well. How could I ever miss that voice and speech style! Their taking Dink was some comfort. I would go through whatever I faced in the hours ahead with a companion and friend, and I knew no one with whom I would rather face such adversity than with good old Dink!

The travel pattern we followed the next hours seemed familiar, not because I could see it, but because we had been through a similar one previously. A ride in the van, and then a plane ride of several hours, and then another van over some rough terrain, until finally we were on a more normal highway. My guess, though I couldn't check it with Dink, because they would not allow us to talk to one another, was that we were being taken back to Comptonville. It was their form of extradition, so we could appear before their kangaroo court. Their method bypassed the normal lengthy and uncertain methods of extradition. Just grab your suspect, take him to your town (it was easier if you were in a small mountain town), and then claim that we had been caught in their area after we had been ordered to leave and never return. Then they could do anything with us they wanted, as far as convicting us of crimes and punishing us for such crimes.

When we were finally in a jail cell, and the doors had clanged shut, and the hoods were off, sure enough it was just Dink and me in our cell. We looked at one another and smiled, as Dink said, "Well, Preacha, here we'se go again! Painted into anudder corner wid no way out, except by da power of God!"

"I can't deny that!" I replied. "I wonder what the charges will be this time? I think you will agree this is their method of extradition, so they can get us in their law court on their choice of charges!"

"Can't argue wid dat, Preacha!" Dink replied. "But at least dey didn't take us back to da death house in da mountains! Not yet, anyways."

"We had just as well get some sleep!" I suggested, as I stretched out on one of the beds in the cell, such as it was. It was creeping towards dawn, and who knew what they had cooked up for us when morning came. There were a few blankets and pillows on the beds before us, and I don't know about Dink, but I was soon asleep, though it was not a deep sleep.

I heard Dink say just moments before I was beyond hearing him, "Preacha, how 'bout some study of da Word?" His voice really didn't sound that eager. My reply was short but honest. "In the morning Dink! In the morning!"

31 What Ever Happened to Holiness?

Because the beds were hard and the sleep was difficult, we both began to stir after a couple of hours in bed. I don't know how long Dink had been awake, when I came to life, but when I saw him stirring, I suggested now was the time for the study of the Word.

In our last session we had traced Israel's fickle heart, when they murmured and complained about the trials, after the great time of rejoicing following the marvelous victory at the Red Sea. So for this day, we turned to the events of Mt. Sinai. Could not God's people be faithful even after such momentous events as the Red Sea victory: the bitter water at Marah becoming sweet; the manna from heaven, when they were hungry; water from the rock, when they had no water again in the desert; and after the great victory over Amalek, wrought by the power of God?

Finally, in their journey they came and encamped before Mt. Sinai, where God very clearly made a covenant with them (Exodus 19). They were told by God that if they would obey His voice and keep His covenant, they would be a peculiar treasure unto Him before all people, because all the earth is the Lord's (verse 3). The people answered together, "All that the Lord says we will do!" Moses then took the words of the people back before the Lord.

God then commanded Moses to sanctify the people (set them apart unto the Lord), and the Lord would come down in the sight of all the people upon the mount on the third day. Moses was also commanded to put a border around the mount, and any one who went up to the mount or touched the mount, would be put to death.

Thus Moses and the people made preparation, as God had commanded. On the third day in the morning there was thunder and lightning, and a thick cloud upon the mount, and the voice of the trumpet (of God) was exceedingly loud, so that all the people in the camp trembled. Then Moses brought the people out from the camp, and they stood at the lower part of the mount. Before their very eyes Mt. Sinai became altogether smoke, because the Lord descended upon the mountain in fire, and the smoke ascended as the smoke of a furnace, and the whole mountain shook greatly! What a scene of God's holy presence this was!

Then the voice of the trumpet sounded even longer and louder and louder, and Moses spoke, and God answered! The Lord called Moses up into the mount, and told him to warn the people once again, lest any break through to try to gaze upon the Lord, for they would perish. Moses was commanded not to let the people break through, nor the priests, but only he and Aaron could come up the mountain.

It was in this context that Moses went up and spoke God's Ten Commandments unto the people. But when the people saw all the thunder and lightning, and heard the voice of the trumpet, and saw the smoking mountain, they backed away, and would not even come near the mount. They told Moses to speak to them, for they did not want God to speak to them, lest they die. Moses told them not to be afraid, for God had come to test them. Moses then drew near to God through the thick darkness, and God gave him instructions and laws for the people. Thus God had given the Ten Commandments, civil laws for the people, and instructions for the building of the tabernacle, and instructions for the worship, which was to take place in the tabernacle.

But it was while Moses was gone a rather lengthy time of forty days and forty nights from the people (Exodus

24:18), receiving the instructions concerning the tabernacle and its worship, that the people showed their hearts once again. These faithless souls, who had seen so much of the grace and power of their God, pressed Aaron to make them idols or gods, because they didn't know what had happened to this man Moses! They had just pledged to obey the commandment that said, "Thou shalt have no other gods before me!" They had been told this in the most reverential setting and fearful atmosphere at the foot of the mount (reverence meaning respect and even a reverential fear). And it was just after the miracle of their deliverance from Egypt, when they saw God's love and care for them in bringing them through the wilderness to the mount!

Where is the faith they claimed as they left Egypt? Where is the faith they should have learned at the Red Sea? Where is the faith, which should have increased, as they came through the wilderness, as God never failed to take care of them and meet their needs, even in the face of the hostile Amalekites? Where is the faith, which should have been strengthened, as they were privileged to experience the presence of God at the mount, as frightening as it may have been?

Is it not sad that they seemed to have learned nothing about faith or the true God of heaven? The first time they are boxed in again, as Moses was gone forty days and forty nights, they fell back into their old ways of doubt and fear and complaining. And even worse, they went back to their former ways of worship, which they had learned in Egypt. Surely, they must have thought, though the Bible does not say this clearly, that the former gods of the Egyptians were more comfortable to be around, than the only true God! What an insult! His holiness scares the living daylights out of them, and His servant cannot be found at this time!

They may have wanted to keep moving---anywhere, just get us out of here. Get us away from this burning mountain and this fearful God and His presence!

Is not this the sense of some even today? They want a comfortable God---no holiness, no demands upon them, no accountability, no judgment, no wrath. Just give them a God Who they can mold to suit themselves; one they can manipulate to do their bidding; one they can worship when they please and as they please with no stringent rules or laws or expectations upon them! Is that not the kind of god many want today?

Do men not say in their own way today, "Let's get away from the holy God of heaven and such a fearful setting! Away with God and his leadership! Away from any reminder of God's holiness! Just let us serve God as we wish! Away with the Biblical God, and let us construct one who suits us! Away with such strict guidelines of holy worship, holy living, holy walking, and holy talking.

We are not making a cry for a return to the days of Israel's existence, but recognition that even in our lives and worship today, there is a need for obedience and holiness before the Lord. Does not the New Testament say in Hebrews 12:14, "Without holiness, no man shall see the Lord?" And, further, does not the New Testament proclaim in I Peter 1:16, "You shall be holy, for I am holy?"

Where did we ever get the idea that we can jettison holiness in our walk before the Lord or in His Church? Or that there can be true faith, where there is no holiness? Or that there be a walk with the Lord in faith, when we compromise so quickly the clear and undeniable necessity of living a godly life as Christians? Have we not been saved unto holiness! Saved not by being holy, but unto holiness? Does not the Scripture say that Christ will save His people "from their sins?" (Matthew 1:21)

Does anyone believe that God forgives us our sins, so that we can go on sinning and walking in an unholy life? Does the Scriptural statement that Christ will save us from our sins, mean only that He will save us from the wrath and judgment upon us because of sin, but not from the reality of sin in our lives? This is not to say that we will be perfect, but that we will be growing and becoming more and more a holy people with a greater and growing faith. Could this not be the reason some have such a weak and wavering faith---because of the lack of holiness in their lives?

Dink must have thought I was running out of gas, as he jumped in, saying, "Preacha, you'se sawin' da wood now---dat's preachin' dat needs ta be done in ever' church. No wonder so many professin' Christians fail so miserably in der lives---preachers fallin' inta blatant sins; lay people livin' double lives, tryin' to straddle da world an da church, hiden' der sins, only ta be exposed eventually. An all dis stains da name of Christ an' His church!"

"You know, Dink!" I picked up the conversation again. "Holy living for many becomes only a desire, when they come to a boxed-in place in their lives. The Lord brings a trial, and there is seemingly no way out. So all of a sudden they seem to become holy and godly---until the trial and boxed-in situation is gone. But how soon they show their true spiritual colors, and return to the old ways, as they become slack and unconcerned about true holy living."

"Dat's right, Preacha! And some claim to be Christians and never have had a holy life. Dey lives like da world, yet usin' da name of Christ fer der benefit, but dey knows nothin' 'bout true Christianity and a holy life! Dat's ole Clark, all right---plus too many others like him!"

32 Where Do We Go from Here?

It wasn't easy to wait in this cell for word as to what was coming next. They did give us an opportunity, after a full day in Comptonville, to call our families and anyone else we desired to contact. We guessed that they gave us that full day with no calls in order to substantiate their claim we had come to Comptonville on our own, and we had not been kidnapped and brought there by them. Then they set a day and time when we would appear before their court---the next day at 10:00 o'clock in the morning.

So we called our families and Mac and Dr. Graham. Mac said he would bring us his best lawyer. No one could believe how we had been shanghaied and taken to Comptonville, but admitted that such might be difficult to prove one way or the other. So our interest turned, not to argumentation that we had been kidnapped, but to the defeat of the charges they would bring against us---whatever those might be. Surprisingly, that afternoon we had an unexpected visitor, none other than Clark Compton himself. It was obvious that he felt he now had the upper hand, as he arrogantly came into the area of our cell, and spoke with a sneering smile.

"Well, are you men ready to give up, yet?" he queried with a sinister laugh. "You surely know you can't win! I will be glad to help you out of this mess, if you agree to certain things!"

Dink and I looked at one another, and then shook our heads, which surely sent a message that we wanted nothing to do with any deal with him. With that he seemed to lose his smile, and suddenly he became very caustic.

"Listen, you scum! Don't you know when you are licked? I control this court and town, and we have it rigged so there is no way you can win---anything! You can't prove you did not come to Comptonville this second time on your own! You can't prove you were not caught breaking into the First Baptist Church in the middle of the night! You can't prove you didn't steal a car in your own hometown of Seminary City and drive it here! You can't prove you were not caught with an unregistered gun! You can't prove you did not slug a police officer of the Comptonville force! Need I name more charges? You are at my mercy! Don't you have enough sense to know when you are beaten? A smart man would be willing to listen to a deal!"

Dink then replied with a confident smile and voice.

"If it would make ya happy, den state yer deal, but I can guarantee ya dat we ain't buyin' it! Fer some reason, we jus' don't tink we can trust da likes a you! An' fer anudder reason, we jus' don't like you, an dat means we knows we ain't gonna like yer deal either. So why doncha jus' go an' sell yer snake oil deals ta someone else dat don't really know ya likes we do!"

I smiled as I watched Clark Compton's response. He was used to getting his own way---always! He was the king of manipulators and power brokers! But now he had met his match in us---men he could not manipulate nor overpower. His reply came with much sarcasm and bitterness.

"Oh, you think you can beat me in this match of power and wits, do you? Go ahead! Try it! I guarantee you that no one has tried and lived to tell it! I will see you either in jail for years to come or in the death house in the mountains or in the death pit! Which do you want? I have made my last offers of compromise with you two!"

33 What's Next in Our Bible Study?

With that outburst Clark Compton stomped out of the jail area. We had won that encounter, but in the process we had enraged the enemy. But we reminded ourselves that he was not battling with us, but with our God, because truth was on our side. Understandably, we were now even more eager to look into the Word of God for strength and support.

We had been following the children of Israel out of the land of Egypt as they journeyed to Palestine, the Promised Land. We know from Scripture that they finally left Mt. Sinai, after their failure there, but God in His grace and mercy still gave them the law, the tabernacle, and the Levitical priesthood, and the tabernacle worship.

We rejoined them in Numbers 13, after they had moved to Kadesh-Barnea, not too great a distance from the Promised Land. From there they sent spies to survey the land, and see what awaited them, as far as the land itself and the number and strength of the people. Twelve spies were sent out in total, including Joshua and Caleb. The report was good news and bad news. The good news consisted of the fact that it truly was a land, which flowed with milk and honey---that is a rich and prosperous land. The bad news was that the people there were strong and they dwelled in walled cities, plus the children of Anak (a strong group of people) dwelled there. Plus, there were the Amalekites, the Hittites, the Jebusites, the Amorites and the Canaanites.

But, the spies were divided, not equally in number, but in their opinions. Caleb said, "Let us go up at once, and possess the land; for we are well able to overcome it." But the men of unbelief said, "We are not able to go up against the people; for they are stronger than we are." Plus, they said, "The land is a land that eats up the inhabitants thereof, and all the people that we saw in it are men of great stature. And we saw the giants there, the sons of Anak, who were born of the giants, and we were in our own sight as grasshoppers, and so we were in their sight."

Thus there were two opposite opinions by people who had all seen the mighty power of their great God to deliver them from Egypt and take them to Mt. Sinai, where they had seen His glory and power once again. Why the difference in this people and their opinions of what they should do at this crucial moment of their lives? Is it not because Joshua and Caleb were looking at the land of promise by faith, and the other ten spies were looking at the land through eyes of unbelief?

But the real question is, who did these people, who all had seen the mighty power of their God during their journey, believe? Did they believe the ten opinions of unbelief or the two men of faith? Sadly, they believed the ten unbelieving spies and not the two men of faith. What a lesson for us! Are not the spiritual people of God usually a minority---even in His church today?

The story now moves us into Numbers 14, and we learn that the entire congregation wept that night! Why? These were not tears of joy and faith, but tears of unbelief, for our text says that they murmured against Moses and Aaron. Unbelief always takes greater comfort and refuge in complaining and crying than in praise and rejoicing in those hours when it seems we are boxed-in by the enemy and dependent on the power of God alone. Listen to their feeble cries and rebellious complaints:

> Would to God that we had died in the land of Egypt!

Would to God that we had died in the wilderness!

The Lord our God has brought us into this land to fall by the sword!

Would it not be better for us to return to Egypt?

Let us make us a captain and return to Egypt!

Could this be possible? They rejected their God? They rejected their leader, Moses? They mutinied to take over from their God-given leadership? They instead made a commitment to depend upon themselves, and to elect their own leader? They pledged dependence to that new leader, so he could get them back to Egypt, while they rejected their dependence upon God to give them the promised land as He promised? Who can believe this?

Who would provide them water on the way? Had they forgotten Marah? Who would defeat the Amalekites? Had they forgotten that battle wrought by God alone? Did they expect God to rubber-stamp their decision to go back to Egypt and their replacement of His leadership with a leader of their own choice, who would no doubt be a man after their own fleshly ways? How irrational is unbelief!

But isn't this what we see so often in God's church today? Churches not looking to God, but giving in to unbelief, when boxed in by the enemy! Or the removal of God-given pastors to turn the reins of leadership over to some self-chosen and unanointed captain to lead by human wisdom and human means and human power?

Surely, these were good words for us on this uncertain day with an uncertain future, as far as men could see or predict!

34 Can You Believe This?

When we finished our study, I got up to stretch and pace the cell a bit. Without thinking I leaned against the cell door, and to my surprise it swung open. Immediately, I called it to Dink's attention.

"Careful, Preacha! Ya can bet dat dey did dat on purpose, so's dat we will try ta escape an maybe even die in da process!"

"Die in the process?" I asked with some shock.

"Yeah, Preacha, an' ya can bet dat dey left a clear path ta escape also. Dey wud want nothin' better dan fer us ta die tryin' ta escape, so dey wouldn't have ta deal wid us even in der court room. And besides dat, where we gonna go if we did escape? Off inta da mountains ta fall inta anudder pit? Or ta be taken ta da cabin agin? Nah! Our safest place is right here in dis jail, an' our best hope is ta face da judge in dat courtroom, when we's gots at least our own lawyer an' Mac present an' maybe other witnesses!"

I must admit that what he said sounded logical, but why then did I wonder if it would really come to pass as he had predicted? Nothing else had gone according to our expectations of the law in this present fiasco. But I reminded my disturbed heart, that even in lawless places, when facing a giant fiasco, our God is still on the throne, and the enemy can do nothing to us except that which has been ordained by God Himself from eternity past. With those comforting words, I spent the rest of the day in thought and meditation concerning the greatness of our God. I fell asleep early that night, trusting Him for tomorrow.

We were rousted out of bed (such as it was) at 5:00 the next morning, and told to clean up, so we could appear before the judge almost immediately. Dink and I both looked at each other, wondering how their court could meet, when we didn't expect our lawyer and Mac to be in Comptonville until about 10:00 AM or so? Or would they take us to court without a lawyer to represent us?

Sure enough! As soon as we were finished showering and were dressed, we were escorted into the courtroom, while it was still dark. Clark Compton was there with several of his lawyers and goons, and the judge was present, as were some of the local police. But our lawyer and Mac were nowhere to be found. It was too early!

Clark Compton's lawyer took about forty-five minutes detailing our supposed crimes, and when they were finished, the judge asked if we had representation. Dink spoke up and tried to present our concerns.

"Yer honor, ain't dis highly irregular fer a court ta meet at 6:00 in da mornin' and 'specially when da counsel fer da defense was told to be here at 10:00 AM?"

"Does that mean that you two men have no defense?" the judge asked.

"No, sir! Dat means we just ain't got no lawyer, cause you's convenin' da court too early!" Dink answered.

"I guess that means that the court will have to provide you a lawyer! Would that be agreeable with you?" the judge said without even looking up.

"No, sir. Dats not goin' ta be agreeable wid us!" Dink answered. "We wants ta wait till 10:00 AM, as agreed, so's our lawyer can be here!"

All the while Clark Compton was sitting in the courtroom, looking bored. Finally he spoke, and it was obvious he was in charge and very impatient.

"Your honor, I am supposed to be somewhere by noon ---somewhere six hours flying time from Comptonville. I am the main speaker at a conference. I suggest these men be allowed to represent themselves. I will be glad to agree to that!"

I thought to myself rather sarcastically, what a mister nice guy this is! He is so sure nothing will make any difference in this kangaroo court, that he graciously wants us to be our own lawyers, just so he can be somewhere on time. As expected, the judge agreed with his suggestion.

Thus we were given two minutes to summarize our defense. Again, my thoughts shocked me---two minutes to summarize our defense, when the other lawyer had forty-five minutes to present the accusations? I was convinced there wasn't any sense for us to try, but then Dink took the floor, regardless of the deck stacked against us!

"You men, an' I mean you, Mr. Judge, an' you, Dr. Compton, may have da power ta do whatever ya wants ta do wid us taday in dis courtroom. But I wants ta tell ya dat der is a Higher Power, Who's watchin' youse men an dese proceedins'. Ya may tink dat plagiarism an' da destruction of a man's life an' ministry after he's dead, an' whatever else you's done in dis town, or whatever you's about ta do ta us, can be hidden an' covered up. But I assure ya dat all tings done in secret will someday be brought ta light, an' dis will come ta light sooner dan you'se tink!

"Ya see, wese gots da finest lawyers in da land buildin' a case against all of ya, and if you'se gets ridda us, you'se just addin' fat ta da fire of yer earthly judgment, let alone yer eternal judgment by da highest judge of all."

I looked at Clark Compton as Dink was speaking, but nothing seemed to faze him. But the judge was something else. He began to twist and turn in his chair, as if he wished to silence Dink at once. When the judge said nothing, Clark Compton spoke up.

"Judge, don't you think this is all unnecessary. He's not presenting a case. He's preaching a sermon. Judge, do your job, and do it now!" he demanded

"Mr. Judge!" Dink continued unphased, "I would be very careful what I did just now! For all ya know, da FBI may meet ya before ya ever gets off dis mountain. An' don't ya know, dat as soon as you's no longer helpful ta Clark Compton, dat yer life ain't worth a plug nickel, an you'll face yer Maker fer His judgment too fer playin' waterboy for ole Clark here all dese years?"

I had to admit that I was quite concerned at this moment. What if the judge took a stand against Clark Compton, and ordered the Comptonville police to arrest him, and then they started to do so, being fed up with him too. Would it be the judge and the local police against Clark and his goons? Or would it be all in the room (except us, of course) against the poor judge?

I could almost see the wheels spinning with such thoughts in the judge's head. Surely, he must have tired down through the years of being a lap dog for Compton. And now it seems Dink had hit a sore nerve in his life. Who would have expected such a thing, and who would have had the nerve to challenge the judge in his own courtroom? Only Dink!

The judge's face went pale, and he began to sweat, and his breathing became heavy from the tenseness of the hour. I really wondered if he was going to have a stroke or a heart attack. And then he did speak!

"My decision is that we reschedule this trial for today at 10:00 AM, when these men have due representation."

With that he slammed his gavel on his desk and exited the room, and he was quickly followed by everyone else. Dink and I were left in the courtroom all by ourselves!

35 Is Der Any Doubt Whose Wid Us?

With a clear courtroom and an unlocked door, I must admit that my first thought again was to try to escape, but Dink must have read my mind for the second time, as he said, "Don't even tink 'bout it, Preacha!"

So we sat down to wait, and since I had my Bible and notebook, we decided to continue our study in Numbers 14. We had seen God's people's further rebellion against Him, as they had desired to go back to Egypt in light of the negative report of ten of the spies they had sent into the Promised Land. They even thought they could elect a new leader to replace Moses to take them back to Egypt. We then took up the story at Numbers 14:11.

Obviously, such action grieved the Lord, and He asked Moses how long this people would provoke Him? And how long it would be before they would believe Him? It is not even made worse in light of all the signs and wonders that God had shown them?

Therefore, because of their unbelief, God said He would smite His people with pestilence and disinherit them, and that He would make of Moses a greater nation mightier than the children of Israel. Oh, the great cost of unbelief to the one who professes to be the child of God! How many blessings have we missed because of unbelief? It reminded me of James 4:2, "You have not because you ask not!" Compare that with Ephesians 3:20, that says our God is able to do exceeding abundantly above all that we are able to ask or think! It is then that one gets an understanding of God's power and willingness to bless, and the place of prayerlessness and the lack of faith which limits His blessings to us, not because of any inability within God, but because of unfaithfulness on our part!

But there was a man of faith in this context of sorrow and unbelief, whose name was Moses. He pled not for himself or for the children of Israel, but for the glory of God. Moses showed his agreement with God, when he acknowledged to God that the Egyptians would hear of the destruction of Israel, and they would tell it to the inhabitants of the Promised Land. These inhabitants had also heard that the Lord was among this people. Had His people not seen the Lord face to face? Had not a special cloud stood over them? Had not the Lord gone before them in a pillar of a cloud by day and a pillar of fire by night?

Then Moses noted that if God killed all this people that the nations would say that He was not able to bring them into the land, which He swore He would give them, and that His inability to give them the land is the reason He killed them in the wilderness. Thus Moses realized two things: 1) that God's glory, which was primary, would be stained, if God killed this people, and, 2) that God was working with this people not for their sake, but for His glory. What a man of faith this Moses---not complaining when in discouraging circumstances, and not wallowing in unbelief, but pleading the glory of God as a reason for God to spare His people. Surely, this was pleasing to the heart of God, as is our faith and our desire for His glory in every situation that we face.

But the work of Moses and the evidence of his growing maturity is not finished. He now prays (see Numbers 14) for the people, as few men have ever prayed. Hear the bold plea of his heart, based on his faith and the glory of God.

> 17 And now, I beseech thee, let the power of my Lord be great, according as thou hast spoken, saying, 18 The Lord is longsuffering, and of great mercy,

forgiving iniquity and transgression, and by no means clearing the guilty, visiting the iniquity of the fathers upon the children unto the third and fourth generation. 19 Pardon, I beseech thee, the iniquity of this people, according unto the greatness of Thy mercy, and as Thou hast forgiven this people, from Egypt even until now.

It was then that the Lord stated His forgiveness of His people's sins, according to the word of Moses. He added that as He lived, all the earth would be filled with His glory! But there was a price for this people to pay! All of those upwards of twenty years of age, who had seen His glory and miracles, which He had performed in Egypt and in the wilderness, and have now put Him to the test these ten times, and have not listened to His voice, will never see the Promised Land! They will die in the wilderness!

Are there not valuable lessons here for us? God does what He does for His own glory, not for our glory or benefit! We can either trust Him and obey Him in the midst of a trial or test, and do His will as He has commanded, and bring Him glory, and see greater things for His glory in the future, or we can refuse to obey Him because of unbelief! But in that case we will miss the fullness of His blessings, not only at one moment in our lives, but maybe even for years to come. Oh, the reward of faith and the loss because of unbelief! Such could (though not always) have lifetime results, if such unbelief is continual and recalcitrant over a period of time!

Dink popped into the conversation with his, "Wow, Preacha! There ain't no doubt what our attitudes gotta be right now, regardless of da circumstances! We'se gots da Lord on our side, an da enemy on da run! All fer His glory! We couldn't be inna better spot dan right here!"

36 Do We Have to Eat Lunch?

With our Bible study finished, and with no return of anyone to the courtroom, we now had a decision to make. Do we just sit tight, or do we look out into the hallway to see if we can learn anything about the whereabouts of everyone? Then all of a sudden, we heard two gunshots!

I looked at Dink again, and he shook his head and stated firmly once again, "Preacha, don't even tink 'bout leavin dis room or lookin' out dat door!" So we just sat quietly in our chairs.

After a few minutes, I looked at the clock on the wall. By now it was almost eight o'clock. I hoped our people would get here soon---even way early! Then the door opened again, and everyone filed in, except Clark Compton and a few of his goons. On the one hand, that made sense, as he had already stated that he had to be in another place by noon. But on the other hand, I didn't look upon him as a guy who would trust the proceedings of this court to the responsibility of another, especially if the judge was wavering.

And then another thought came to me! If everyone was in the courtroom besides Clark and a few of his men, what were the shots all about? Had there been a mutiny outside the courtroom, and were those bullets for Clark and one of his men? Or were they just to trying to flush us out so they could be rid of us without a trial, like Dink thought they might be doing? (We found out later that was the case!)

But now before the judge could crack his gavel, Mac and our lawyer walked in the door. I don't think I have ever been so glad to see anyone in all my life. The judge tried to welcome them, but even at doing that, he appeared a little antsy and uncertain of what he was doing, or maybe it was what he should do now! Had Mac and our lawyer's entrance thrown a monkey wrench into their little plans?

Finally, he smacked the desk with his gavel, took a deep breath, and made a very unexpected announcement.

"I am sorry to inform you all that this hearing must be postponed, as Dr. Compton, the chief witness against these men, has an appointment elsewhere at this hour. We will reschedule this for next week at this same time!"

And with that he hit the desk again with his gavel, got up, and walked out the door, even though our lawyer tried to address him. No questions allowed, no answers given---just a postponement, which meant we probably would spend another week in the friendly confines of the Comptonville jail.

The Comptonville police surrounded us, and told us we were gong back to our cell. But I asked, "Without even talking to our lawyer?"

One little smart-aleck cop answered, "Yeah, without even talking to your lawyer!" It was then that our lawyer got into it, reminding the officers of their illegal actions of kidnapping us, and of their failure to allow us counsel, which was a clear violation of our rights. With no judge around to rule, the police finally gave us permission to see our lawyer---but only for five minutes they said. Then Mac gave us the bad news!

"Well, he's done it! Clark Compton now owns half of Turnover News Agency, as my brothers sold their stock to him, which now makes him an equal partner with me. And he has warned me that if I publish anything about him or the alleged plagiarism, he will sue me and break me in the battle to get control of TNA!"

I looked at Dink, and he was shaking his head, as was Mac, and even our lawyer. About that time Dr. Graham, the president of our seminary, walked in the door. He was still quite early for our 10:00 AM meeting! We told him of all the events, as quickly as we could, before they took us back to our cell. He stood there with his mouth open, trying to figure out a way to protest it all, as we had been doing. As we parted, they said they would spend the day, and see if they could see us again, before they had to leave town.

When we got back to our jail cell, we were too exhausted even to study, though we needed to challenge our hearts at this juncture. Our box was getting tighter---that one which had us stymied and penned in. We both prayed about the situation, as we stretched out on our beds exhausted! We weren't even recovered by the noon hour, when our meal was delivered to us.

We tried to tell the man delivering the food, we were not hungry, but he insisted that we take the food. Who felt like eating at a time like this? Then the delivery man said as he left, "Be sure and read the note inside your piece of chicken, if you want some encouragement!"

I grabbed my tray of food, and got it out of sight as best I could, and tore open my piece of chicken, and sure enough, there was a note in it! I opened it quickly and read it in a whisper, so Dink could hear it.

"You have nothing to worry about! I have something that will sink the Compton ship! Wish I could tell you! No one knows about it but me right now! But others will soon! And it will be the end of the Compton kingdom! Just be patient! And be sure and destroy this note! And by the way, I am alive and well---never better!"

The note was signed---George Carlson!

37 How Are Moses and Israel Doing?

We certainly had a lot to talk about, after George Carlson had surprised us with his smuggled note. The food even tasted better than usual. Plus, we had all kinds of unanswered questions. What was the news he had, which he didn't reveal to us? Where had he been all this time? How did he get to be the food deliveryman? Would he deliver supper that night, so we could ask him some questions?

All these events, though there were some unanswered questions still, made our afternoon study much more meaningful. We turned to Numbers 14 again, beginning at verse 39, to see the strange response of the people to God's reaction to their refusal to enter the Promised Land.

When God's people heard the final result of their unbelief, that they would die in the wilderness, and would not have the privilege of entering into the Promised Land, they sought to take matters into their own hands again. They rose up early in the morning and went to the top of the mountain and reported to Moses that they were now ready to go up to the land God had promised. Plus, they admitted that they had sinned!

Moses asked them why they transgressed the command of the Lord? And he told them their actions would not prosper them. He commanded them not to go up, because the Lord was not among them! They will therefore fall before their enemies! They shall be smitten by the Amalekites and Canaanites, and will be slain by the sword! Why? Because they have turned away from the Lord, and therefore, the Lord will not go with them.

But would you believe it, they decided to go up anyway and try to conquer the land---without the Lord! The Bible says they presumed to go up! That is, they thought they could do this without the Lord by their own strength, and even without Moses and the ark of the covenant, which stayed in the camp behind them. But the Amalekites and the Canaanites smote them and even routed them!

Has there ever been such a blatant act of rebellion against God? Has there ever been such a blind trust in self and man's power? Has there ever been such a blindness to the truth of God and the reality of one's own sin? All coming from those who are supposed to be the people of God? As our friend CHM says:

> Nature [human nature] may rush into the scene of operation; but God does not want it there. It must be withered, crushed, set aside. The place of death is the place for [human] nature. If it [human nature] will be active, God will so order matters, in his infallible faithfulness and perfect wisdom, that the results of its activity will prove utter defeat and confusion. He [God] knows what to do with [human] nature, where to put it, and where to keep it. (Mackintosh, *Genesis to Deuteronomy*, p. 145)

> How hard it is to overcome the unbelief of the human heart! How difficult man ever finds it to trust God! How slow he [man] is to venture upon the naked promise of Jehovah! Anything for nature, but that. The most slender reed that the human eye can see is counted more substantial, by far, as a basis for nature's confidence than the unseen "Rock of ages." Nature will rush avidly to any creature stream or broken cistern, rather than abide by the unseen "Fountain of living waters." (Mackintosh, p. 159)

> Unbelief is not humility, but thorough pride. It refuses to believe God because it does not find in self a reason for believing. This is the very height of presumption. If, when God speaks, I refuse to believe, on the ground of something in myself, I make Him a liar, and exhibit the inherent pride of my heart. [I would add---for a person not to believe because he sees nothing in God as the ground of faith, is equally to make God a liar and exhibit the great pride of the human heart.] (Mackintosh, p. 161)

Dink spoke up, when he saw I was finished.

"I wonder, Preacha, if we ain't been guilty of dat same ting our brother is writin' about? We was down in da dumps, based on some change of venue by da court, an' den we got all excited an' encouraged by what George Carlson said ta us, when we don'ts even know what he's talkin' 'bout! Was we trustin' in human reason rather dan in God's promise?"

"I see your point Dink! But can't faith in God still be grounded on God, and yet our hearts be encouraged by any sign which might point to God's promise being fulfilled?"

"Yeah, but how 'bout bein' discouraged when der ain't no sign His promise is bein' fulfilled?" Dink asked again.

"I see your point, Dink! And I think I might have been guilty! Lord, forgive us, for allowing our emotions and the things we can see and the things we cannot see influence us in our faith and trust in You and your promises!" I said as we closed our session in prayer.

The supper question was answered shortly thereafter, when our food was delivered. It was not George, and the deliveryman assured us that he had delivered the noon meal! Thus George's work was a one-meal job!

38 You Made a Deal for Us?

As I woke up the next morning, I wondered what this new day would bring. Life is so uncertain, as far as the detailed events, but it is not uncertain as to who is in charge. The Lord God Omnipotent reigneth! It seemed like a very normal day. Too normal when one is in jail. Nothing new, so we thought!

But to our surprise we were summoned back into the courtroom about 1:00 in the afternoon, having no idea what to expect next. But again to our surprise, our lawyer, and Dr. Graham, and Mac were present, when we walked through the door. But then, Clark Compton was there also. I guess he had gotten his speech over from yesterday, and could spare us this day from his busy schedule, I thought sarcastically.

I looked at Mac, and he gave me a thumbs up, which I took to mean good news, but I had no idea what that good news was, Finally, the judge entered, and we all stood, and after we were seated, the procedures began.

"Will the defendants please rise!" the judge instructed.

I wondered if he was going to pass sentence upon us, and give us more days in jail, but then that couldn't be good news, as indicated by Mac.

"It is my duty to inform you, Mr. Pointer and Mr. Dink, that you are free to go, as long as you will abide by the agreement which has been tendered between Dr. Compton and Mac Turnover. Since they both now own fifty percent of Turnover News Agency, in light of the recent acquisition by Dr. Compton of an equal number of shares, it is my duty to inform you of their agreement. If you will agree to abide by the terms of the agreement, then you too can benefit and be set free from the charges against you. The agreement stipulates the following: 1) that Mac Turnover will continue to have management control and authority over TNA, as long as he does not write, or discuss, or communicate in any manner the accusations which have surfaced once again about Dr. Clark Compton having plagiarized the books which are now attributed to his name; 2) that Dr. Compton will drop all charges against Mr. Pointer and Mr. Dink, as long as they too agree to cease from their efforts to harass Dr. Compton concerning the above mentioned accusation of plagiarism!"

I looked at Dink, and then at Mac, and wondered if he knew something we did not how. Had he given up on exposing Clark Compton? Were we going to let him get away with plagiarism and even possibly murder, just to save our own skins? This was surely something I had not expected. I would have given a pretty good sum for Dink's thoughts on the matter right now. Why not ask if Dink and I can discuss this with our lawyer, or at least with one another? And so I did, and, surprisingly, we were allowed to talk among ourselves and to our lawyer.

We were told that this was the only way they could think of to get us out of jail, and because they did not know how dangerous it might be there, they thought they had better push this deal---for our sake. This did not mean that we were finished with Clark Compton, nor were we giving up on putting him behind bars, though we did not tell his lawyer that.

But neither Dink nor I were comfortable with the deal, and so we rejected it! By doing this we put the ball back in their court! They had illegally arrested us, and such was known to our lawyer and others. The ball was in their court now!

39 What Will They Do with Us Now?

As Dink and I went back to our cell, we wondered what would be next? Would they see the foolishness of keeping us and let us go? Or would they detain us in jail, while they tried to figure out what to do with us? Dink predicted that within an hour, they would let us go! Too risky for them to keep us was his guess! Too many people knew we were there! No freedom to do with us as they wished!

Soon the answer came just as Dink had said! All charges were dropped against us (I would have been happier if they would have said they were false charges), and we were free to go! It was clarified, however, that the battle with TNA was still on from the perspective of Clark Compton. Evidently, they thought that was an easier battle for them to win.

When I shared these thoughts with Dink, he added, "Yeah, but maybe deys either scared a keepin' us here, or dey may tink it would be easier ta eliminate us somewhere else in some other way!"

I gulped at that second suggestion, knowing there was a lot of lonely roads between Comptonville and civilization! I told Dink, "I hope it's the first one!"

As we traveled home, I tried to summarize this whole situation for Dink and my thinking, so we would not miss anything.

I noted the following items which were still before us:

1. This all began when William Sangster V came to me to see if he could write a dissertation on his great-great-grandfather's theology.

2. His mother had died at his birth, and he had been adopted at a very young age, and his real father, William Sangster IV, was not known to him until just several months ago.

3. When he had finally found his real father, he had told him the story of his great-great grandfather, William Sangster, Sr. Dr. Sangster had not only been a preacher, who had pastored the First Baptist Church of Comptonville, but he had also written a number of books, mostly commentaries on books of the Bible.

4. But strangely enough there was no longer any record of this man or his ministry in Comptonville, where he had ministered for so long.

5. We had come to several conclusions through our investigation of the situation. Primarily, that Clark Compton, the son of the man who had owned most of the town of Comptonville, and who now himself was running the affairs of Comptonville, was also very dishonest in his other occupation, as he served as the president of a seminary.

6. He had risen to that position by plagiarizing the writings of William Sangster, Sr., and publishing these works in his own name. Furthermore, he had sought to destroy the few books which remained of William Sangster, Sr., who had published them and tried to sell them. But Clark Compton's father, although acting as if he would help market the books, actually sought to destroy them.

7. Now the roof was falling in on the Compton empire, as the great-great-grandson of William Sangster and George Carlson were seeking to expose the dishonesty of the Compton family, with the help of Dink and I, plus Mac and the Turnover News Agency.

8. But the Clark Compton empire was not fading without a fight, as they had sought to keep the boat of their dishonesty afloat very successfully for many years past. But, now, Compton and his cronies were in deep trouble, mainly, because the Turnover News Agency was going to write an article on the whole mess.

9. When Clark Compton couldn't get rid of us in any other way, even after trying literally to eliminate us, he finally arranged a takeover, or as close to it as he could get, of the Turnover News Agency. He had bought the stock of Mac Turnover's two brothers, which made him now an equal partner in TNA with Mac himself.

10. His present goal was to do anything he could to keep the story of his plagiarism from going public, and to that end he had us put in jail in Comptonville on false charges. But when we wouldn't agree to his compromise, which would have kept us from continuing our investigation, he decided it might be better to free us, before our story hit the news big time, exposing him. He figured he could deal with us better away from Comptonville, even if it was in the law courts.

11. We had some friends who were willing to help us in this whole mess. Besides William Sangster V, there was George Carlson, a boyhood friend to Clark Compton, who had given us a complete set of the Sangster books. He had also promised to be there for us at any trial, even with further evidence, that he claimed would turn the tide against Clark Compton. But in reality, no one at this time was quite sure what the evidence was or where he was!

12. There was also a policeman on the Comptonville police department, who had indicated that he wanted to help us, just so he could get out from under the stern authority and criminal actions of Clark Compton. And there was an old friend of Dink's from the Almandine, Ronnie Filmore, who Dink thought might have indicated a desire to talk to him, but they never had the opportunity.

Along with all of this, there was our study of the Word of God, which had kept us going through this dark trial, which also reminded me, that it was time for us to look at the Word of God, even before we arrived home. But above all, there was our great God, who we were trusting to put all these pieces together, somehow, for His glory!

40 What Do We Do Now?

As we continued to travel, having summarized the situation which was before us, Dink asked a question concerning our recent study of the Word of God.

"Preacha, I'se been readin' da story of da children of Israel at Kadesh-barnea agin, an I came 'cross some verses which seems ta contradict one anudder. Now I knows dat da Bible don't have no contradictions, so maybe ya can help me on dese two difficult verses---Numbers 13:1-3 and Deuteronomy 1:19-22."

He then read them to me as follows:

Numbers 13:1-3

> And the Lord spoke unto Moses, saying, 'Send thou men that they may search out the land of Canaan, which I give unto the children of Israel: of every tribe of their fathers shall you send a man, every one a ruler among them.' And Moses by the commandment of the Lord sent them from the wilderness of Paran.

Deuteronomy 1:19-20

> And when we departed from Horeb, we went through all the great and terrible wilderness, which ye saw by the way of the mountain of the Amorites, as the Lord our God commanded us; and we came to Kadesh-barnea. And I said unto you, 'Ye are come unto the mountain of the Amorites, which the Lord our God doth give unto us. Behold, the Lord thy God hath set the land before thee; go up and possess it, as the Lord God of thy fathers hath said unto thee; fear not, neither be discouraged.' And ye came near unto me everyone of you, and said, 'We will send men before us, and they shall search us

> out the land, and bring us word again by what way we must go up, unto what cities we shall come.

"Now here's da problem, Preacha! Numbers says da Lord told Moses ta send da spies, while Deuteronomy says dat da people said dey were gonna send out da spies. Who sent out da spies---da Lord or da people?"

"Well, Dink, if you will get my copy of CHM on the Pentateuch, and turn to his comments on Numbers 13 and read them to yourself first, and then read them to me, we can discuss it. You might get some help on what I have underlined."

It wasn't often that Dink was silent, but he was as he searched out the answer to his own question. Finally, he began reading as follows several quotes from Mackintosh.

> Now here we have the moral root of the fact stated in Numbers 13:2. It is evident that the Lord gave the commandment concerning the spies, because of the moral condition of the people. Had they been governed by simple faith, they would have acted on the soul-stirring words of Moses, 'Behold, the Lord thy God hath set the land before thee; go up and possess it, as the Lord God of thy fathers hath said unto thee; fear not, neither be discouraged.' There is not a single syllable about spies in this splendid passage. What does faith want of spies, when it has the word and the presence of the living God? If Jehovah had given them a land, it must be worth having. And had He not? Yes, truly, and not only, but He had borne testimony to the nature and character of that land in the following glowing words: 'For the Lord thy God bringeth thee into a good land, a land of brooks of water, of fountains, and depths that spring out of the valleys and

hills; a land of wheat and barley and vines and fig-trees and pomegranates; a land of olive oil and honey; a land where in thou shalt eat bread without scarceness, thou shalt not lack any thing in it; a land whose stones are iron, and out of whose hills thou mayest dig brass. (Deuteronomy 8:7-9) (Mackintosh, *Genesis to Deuteronomy, pp. 503-504*)

Should not all this have sufficed for Israel? Ought they not to have been satisfied with the testimony of God? Had not He spied out the land for them, and told them all about it? And was not this enough? What need of sending men to spy out the land? Did not God know all about it? Was there spot from Dan to Beersheba with which He was not perfectly acquainted? Had he not selected this land and allotted it, in His own eternal counsels, of the seed of Abraham His friend. Did He not know all about the difficulties: and was He not able to surmount them? Why, then, did they come near everyone of them, and say, 'We will send men before us, and they shall search us out the land, and bring us word again? (Mackintosh, p 504)

These questions come home right to our hearts. They find us out, and make thoroughly manifest where we are. It is not for us to sit down and coolly animadvert [criticize] upon the ways of Israel in the wilderness, to point out error here and failure there. We must take all these things as types set before us for our admonition. They are beacons erected by a friendly and faithful hand, to warn us off from the dangerous shoals, quicksands, and rocks, which lie along our course, and threaten our safety? (Mackintosh, p 504)

Did not the Lord expressly command Moses to send spies. And if so, how was it wrong for Israel to send them? True, the Lord did command Moses to send the spies, in Numbers 13, but this was in consequence of the moral condition of the people, as set forth in Deuteronomy 1. We shall not understand the former unless we read it in the light of the latter. We learn most distinctly from Deuteronomy 1:22 that the idea of sending the spies had its origin in the heart of Israel. God saw the moral condition, and He issued a command in full keeping therewith. (Mackintosh, p. 504)

There can be no question in the mind of any spiritual person who studies the entire subject, as to the fact that the scheme of sending the spies was the fruit of unbelief. A simple heart that trusted God would never have thought of such a thing. What! Are we to send poor mortals to spy out a land which God has graciously given to us, and which He has so fully and faithfully described? Far be the thought. Nay, rather let us say, It is enough: the land is the gift of God and for such it must be good. His word is enough for our hearts; we want no spies; we seek for no mortal testimony to confirm the word of the living God. He has given; He has spoken; this is enough! (Mackintosh, pp. 504-505)

But, alas! Israel was not in a condition to adopt such language. They would send spies. They wanted them; their hearts craved them; the desire for them lay in the very depths of the soul. Jehovah knew this, and hence He issued a commandment in direct reference to the moral state of the people. (Mackintosh, p. 505)

I also noted for Dink the further illustration that CHM used, which was a similar situation, where God considered the moral condition of the people and allowed their desire to stand though it cost them very dearly in the years to follow. (Mackintosh, p. 504) In I Samuel 8:22 the Lord commanded Samuel to hearken to the voice of the people, and God gave them Saul for a king, because their unbelieving hearts wanted a king! It was not that God approved of their desire, but God allowed their desire to come to fruition to teach them the error of their ways, and even, perhaps, to punish them for their unbelief. As CHM says, "Their king proved a most complete failure, and they [the people] had to learn that it was an evil and bitter thing to forsake the living God and lean on a broken reed of their own selection." (Mackintosh, p. 504)

And we must add that this was a lesson that the children of Israel had to learn as they stood in unbelief before the promised land and desired to send out spies. God said they could do so, not because He agreed with their desire, but so that they would learn (and we and generations to follow would learn) the results of unbelief!

Dink jumped in again with his comments saying, "Boy, Preacha, when youse is messin' wid unbelief of our great God, you just ain't messin' 'round wid triflin' tings. Unbelief is ta call God a liar! He ain't gonna do what He said He would do, we is sayin' He ain't gonna do what He said He would do, cause we is saying dat He is either a liar or he is too weak an' powerless! Wow! Either one a dose accusations 'gainst God by word or action sure is serious stuff---all da results of unbelief! How Israel musta regretted dis moment fer da years ta follow!"

Then Dink prayed for us. "Lord, I believes You is gonna get da victory fer us! Not cause we is anybody, but because You is da mighty God of da universe!"

41 They Did What?

It took us several days again to recuperate from our most recent excursion to jail-land in Comptonville, to say nothing of the time we owed our families. We tried to get away from any thought of what might be Clark Compton's next move against us---at least for awhile!

Finally, I went back to my office at school, thankful that Dr. Graham understood what we had been through, and that he was not pressing us to get back to our school responsibilities. I had not been in my office long that morning until Dink called, and it wasn't good news.

"Preacha, I didn't wanna bother ya long as you was home wid da family, but I saw yer car here dis mornin'. We's gots some more bad news. You'll never guess what ole Clark Compton's done now! Somebody stole da William Sangster books from da storage facility wheres we'se had dem fer safe keepin', an it had ta be him! Whatta scoundrel!"

"You mean someone just walked in, broke down the gates to the facility and the doors to our rented space, and then took all the books we had stored there?" I asked in unbelief?

"Yep, dey beat up da night watchman, took a truck in, an' cleaned da place out---didn't leave a single volume a da Sangster books!"

"Were the police called to the scene of the crime?" I asked again.

"Yep, but dey don't have any idea what happened an' why it happened! Said it musta been some vandals just lettin' off some steam or sumpthin' like dat! I tried ta tell dem different, but dey didn't seem ta want ta hear 'bout it! All it was ta dem was just some old useless books dat was stolen! Dey had no idea of da situation. But it's on da police record, just in case we might needs it in da future!"

"Well, Dink, where does that leave us now? What evidence do we have, as strong as those books, which prove the plagiarism of Compton?" I thought out loud.

"We ain't got no evidence, unless somebody's got anudder set a dem books, an' who could dat be?"

"Which means," I continued, "that if we have no evidence of plagiarism, we have no case against Clark Compton; which means that we become the false accusers and wrongful aggressors against him; which means further that we have no hope of nailing him for any of his crimes from the past years. And any case we thought we had against him in his involvement with Mac becomes weak, and his actions will be seen as nothing but shrewd investment practices on his part and sour grapes on Mac's part! Which also means that he can nail us for any kind of wrongdoing he wants to pursue, and we have no defense against his false accusations! Dink, how did we let ourselves get caught in this one! Shouldn't we have been more careful with those books? And, besides, who told him where we had the books hidden?"

"Youse got it analyzed right, Preacha! Maybe we was jus' too busy wid da house an' da pit an' bein' in jail, dat we missed sometin' dat we shoulda seen commin'!" he stated mournfully.

"Well, Dink, I guess the Lord is just setting things up so that when this is all over, He will surely get the glory, as we have been seeing in Exodus! We can't give in to unbelief now, when we are so close to the promised land of solving this case---to the Lord solving it, I should say!"

"I'll be right over ta yer office, Preacha, so's we can study da Word again! God has da answer!"

42 What Is So Bad About Unbelief?

It wasn't but a few minutes till Dink was in my office ready to think on the subject of faith once again. We had just been dealt another setback in this battle with the enemy. Had it not been true that each time we thought we were making headway in our battle with Clark Compton, something had come along, which seemed to make a final victory more difficult and even more impossible, if that's possible?

I thought we might look at the verse in Hebrews 11, which says that faith is the substance of things hoped for, the evidence of things not seen. Does this not mean that faith does not need evidence of that which God is going to do in the future, but faith in the promise of God is substance enough for us? Does this not indicate that we should not look to the evidence around us that God is or can or will work, but that we are to look to Him and His promise, even when there is no visible evidence or hope that He will work to fulfill His promise? Does this not mean that our eyes should be on God and our faith should be in Him (His person and power and promise), rather than on men or circumstances or human resources, which we or someone else can provide for us?

Thus if we know who God is, and if we are convinced God is Who He says He is in His Word, and if we are convinced that God can and will do what He says He will do, and if God has sworn Himself to us today as He says, then unbelief is the most horrendous of all reactions to God's dealings with us, whether it be a trial or a sorrow or a difficulty in our lives! As we think about unbelief, we must ask, how could we ever be guilty of such a response to God? How great a sin unbelief must be! To doubt God!

To call God a liar! To be so blind as to God's nature and person and promises! To listen to such lies about God as raised by the enemy! To think so irrationally about God! To exaggerate the ability and power of the enemy in comparison to God! I ask again, how can a child of God ever succumb to such things that we have just stated?

That is not to say that one who doubts God in a trial is not saved, unless that pattern of life is overwhelmingly obvious and persistently obstinate and unchangeably ingrained in a person's life and actions over a period of time. We all have to learn the lessons of faith! That God is Who He is! That God can and will do what He says in His Word! That unbelief is sin of the worst kind! That God is a God Who cannot, has not, and will not lie to us! That God is never to be doubted! That the enemy would seek to seal our hearts so many times against God and His will and leadership in our lives, through his lies to us---even about God Himself! That the enemy would even want us to murmur against God and exaggerate the difficulty of the trial before us! That God wants us to trust Him, and though we see the trial, His desire is that we focus our eyes on Him, instead of on the trial itself, in order that we might see the victory But instead of focusing upon God and His promises, how easy to focus on the enemy and stumble all over the place!

Is this not what happened to Korah and his murmuring band of rebels, who came to Moses in Numbers 16? They had no doubt been grumbling and complaining from the time they left Egypt! They had been in agreement with every case of discontentment and unbelief, which had raised its head as Israel traveled under Moses' leadership! Finally, their spirit of irrational discontentment, which exaggerated every trial before them, came to a head in the wilderness, as they confronted Moses to complain.

They accused Moses of taking too much upon himself, and not giving them more say in the governing of the people. They wanted Moses to know that they too were spiritual men, and God was with them, and Moses needed to consult them more. The Lord must have smiled, as He told Moses He would show him tomorrow who was holy and who was not, and who were really His! Then Moses rebuked them, but it didn't do any good, for the characteristics of blatant unbelief includes a recalcitrant heart, which thinks falsely it is right, when it is wrong!

The next day Moses stood and told the people, including Korah and his band of rebels, that they would know that God had not sent him, if these men (Korah and his followers) died a natural death. But if the earth opened its mouth and swallowed them, then they will understand that these men have provoked the Lord, as they have stood against God's leader. Surely, we can all guess what happened! The ground, which was under them, split open, and swallowed them up, along with their houses and all their goods. Then all of the children of Israel ran for their lives, fearing that the same thing might happen to them!

Do we not see how these rebels had given in to the enemy's lies of unbelief? Do we not see how blind and irrational their unbelief was in light of all they had seen of God and His person and power? Do we not see in them how unbelief murmurs and complains against God and His leadership of His people? Do we not see how prideful unbelief can be even to exaggerate one's own importance, as well as the circumstances that displease it?

As our Brother CHM has said, "There is nothing under heaven so stupidly irrational as unbelief!"

43 When Faith Is Not Faith?

Although it was the last thing I expected this day, the phone rang in my office, right after we had finished our study, and a voice said Clark Compton was in town and wanted to talk to me again! I told whomever it was speaking for Clark Compton, yes, on one condition---if I could bring someone with me to confirm what we discussed. After a few minutes, which time was spent, I was sure, getting permission from Compton himself, I was told I could bring one person with me. Thus forty-five minutes later we were headed for a hotel in town to meet with our adversary.

He was not as friendly nor as bouncy in personality as he was the first time we met, but he tried to be friendly and cordial. Since it was his meeting, Dink and I had decided to let him do the talking, until he broached a subject that needed an answer. After the normal greetings, we waited for him to open the subject of conversation.

"I called you men together today, because I don't understand why we cannot come to some agreement on the subject that seems to be bothering you. After all, we are all men of faith, and we do serve the same Lord, and there should be some ground of agreement upon which we can build a relationship of friendship and cordiality for the service of our God!"

As he was talking, I wondered, where one should begin to tackle a statement like that---a statement full of assumptions and even lies!

Then he added with a smile and in a kidding voice, "Who knows when I might need two good teachers at our school---one in evangelism and the other in theology!"

I must admit that I almost lost my lunch on that statement! What a condescending comment! Who did he think he was kidding? We had no interest in teaching at his school, nor did he have any interest in our being there! The statement simply indicated that he would go to any length to quiet us! He had tried intimidation and threats of lawsuits, and now he was going the sugary route of false promises, which bordered on bribery! I couldn't let this hypocrisy pass unchallenged.

"I beg your pardon, sir, but I would ask you in response to your statement, what you think a man of faith is, especially in light of what we have been through the past several weeks?"

He continued with the false smile, as he said, "Well, we all know that a man of faith is a man of the church, who has professed his faith in Jesus---something I did as a young boy many years ago. That was followed by baptism, and then I was faithful in attendance at church through my teenage days. That was followed by college, a Christian college, and then to seminary, which was followed by teaching in Christian schools---a college and then a seminary. Now, as you know, I have been president of a seminary for a number of years. My record there is impeccable and beyond question!"

"But doesn't the Bible say that faith without true Christian works is dead, for even the devil believes (head knowledge) and trembles? And does not the Bible tell us that a person's life tells us something of the truth or falsity of his claimed relationship with Christ? And from what I know of you and your treatment of us and others, your profession of faith in Christ leaves many questions!"

He began to squirm in his chair, and I knew he wasn't happy with such direct confrontational questions. When he sat dumfounded for a few moments, I continued.

"What about your holding us captive those days, after we visited you in your office? What about your men giving us a choice to stay in that house and die of old age, or leave the house in the mountains and die in a few days! No one else had ever gotten out alive, they said! What about the pit, where no one knows how long we would have been there, had not someone rescued us from that place? Is all of that part of your good Christian works?

"What about your takeover of Turnover News Agency in an attempt to shut someone up, who was ready to expose the truth about your sinful past? And what about William Sangster and his writings, which you plagiarized and rode to a teaching vocation in a Christian college, and then on to a seminary, and even all the way to the presidency of that seminary? And what about the elimination of Sangster's life and ministry, as he was removed from the records of First Baptist Church of Comptonville? Can you honestly sit there before God and claim to be a man who possesses true faith in Jesus Christ, which has been proven by true Christian works?"

He tried to be cordial still, but it was obvious he was steaming inside, as he stated, "But the same Bible says to judge not lest you be judged! It also says that a man stands or falls to his own master---not to another human being!" He had walked right into my trap, as he had given me verses I expected!

"Judge not lest you be judged does not mean we cannot make spiritual judgments! If that were the case we could judge nothing---period! Your interpretation of that verse is far too broad, for the Bible says elsewhere that we are to make spiritual judgments! The Bible says to judge not according to appearance, but to make spiritual judgments! See John 7:24. I would not make an eternal judgment concerning you, nor would I judge you only by your appearance as a seminary president! But I would make some spiritual judgments concerning your life---that it falls far short of what a Christian character should be according to the Bible. Your life reminds me of the man who asked the preacher if he could be a Christian gangster, because you are more that than you are a Christian gentleman!"

I could see him fuming under his stoic seminary president's front, as he said, "Don't you dare judge my profession of faith!"

I answered quickly, "I hope you are not one of so many who have a faith in faith! Some seem to say, 'I believe because it makes me feel good to think I believe and to think I am all right!' But I would caution you, do not put your faith in your faith, for that is no faith at all. That is only faith in yourself, which is no faith which saves. The value of faith is not that you think you have it, or that such thinking makes you feel good, or that it causes some church to accept you as a member. The value and evidence of a true faith is that its object is Christ Himself, and not just that you say you have faith. When you have true faith you have Christ, and you are not just forgiven of your sins, but He brings a change to your life, whereby you will grow in His righteousness and godliness. And if one does not evidence His righteousness and godliness in his life, it evidences that one has no true faith at all!"

With that he got up and started to walk out of the room, but he fired one final salvo on his way out, saying, "Well, I guess you don't have much of a case without those books, do you? See you in court!"

44 Do You Want the Books?

When we left Clark Compton, I went back to school to let Dink off, so he could get his car and head home. But when we pulled up under the tree, where he was parked, someone was waiting for us. It was Ronnie Filmore, one of Compton's men---the one who Dink had known years ago in the Almandine! The atmosphere at first, as they met, was strained, because neither one trusted the other, and rightfully so on Dink's part.

Finally, Dink broke the ice when he asked, "Well, what does ya want here wid us, Ronnie? I didn't tink we had anyting ya wanted except da books. I'd bet you waz in on dat caper! What'd ya do wid dem, anyway?"

"Calm down, Dink! I need your help! I know this thing with Clark Compton is coming down on him! He may think he can squirm out of it like he has escaped so many things in the past, but he's never met two guys as persistent as you and Dr. Pointer here!"

"So, what's ya wanta do, Ronnie? Save yer good fer nothin' hide by makin' a deal wid us?" Dink said scornfully. I wondered if he was being a little hard on Ronnie, but he knew him better than I did.

"Ya tell me 'bout da Sangster books, if ya means business 'bout breakin' wid ole Clark! Who took dem an' where are dey now?" Dink demanded to know.

"They were supposed to have been destroyed!" Ronnie informed us. "That way there's no chance of anyone ever getting their hands on them again to use as evidence against Compton. That's the way he works! He leaves no trace of having had his hands on anything illegal. But I was the one who stole them, and he only thinks they have been destroyed. I have them and they are well hidden!"

"But how does I know you'se gots dem?" Dink fired back. "Ya may be playin' da con man now?"

With this Ronnie reached into a brief case and pulled out one of the Sangster books and showed it to us. But Dink, rightfully so, was not convinced.

"How does I know dis aint't just a single copy dat you'se saved from da books we had?" Dink said sarcastically! "An' now ya wants to make us tink ya gots dem all, so ya can get outta dis mess yer in wid Compton?"

"I will deliver them all to you tomorrow evening, and more!" said Ronnie.

"Whaddaya mean, and more?" Dink asked.

"Wait and see!" Ronnie insisted.

"An what does ya want in return?" Dink queried.

"My life!" he replied.

"Whaddaya mean by dat!" Dink asked again.

"I mean my life! I have been pegged for elimination by Clark and his men!" Ronnie explained.

"But how can we stop dat?" Dink asked again.

"I'll tell you tomorrow evening!" he promised, and with that he left.

"Well, what do you think of that exchange?" I asked Dink, as we were left alone again.

"I tink he's either connin' us fer ole Clark, or he's desperate an' really does want out!" Dink noted. "In fact, we may get da books or we may never see him agin!"

I didn't want to get my hopes up too high, but we both realized it would be a great advantage, if we could go into court with a set of those books! But we had been on such a roller coaster ride before of hopes raised and hopes dashed that I reminded myself that the battle was the Lord's, and either way He was still in control.

Maybe I had learned something in all of this after all!

45 Should Not Faith Overcome Fear?

After our discussion with Ronnie Filmore, Dink and I decided to go into my office and study the subject we had been pursing together---our mighty God and the necessity of our faith as we seek to do His will in our lives. We had followed God's people out of Egypt, past the experiences at Mt. Sinai, then up to Kadesh-barnea and their unbelief there, which resulted in their wandering in the wilderness, until a new generation had come. Following the events of their wandering in the wilderness, God spoke to them once again, assuring them that His plan for them to enter the Promised Land had not failed, though the previous generation had failed to claim His promise.

Moses had been allowed to view the land, but he would not be permitted to enter the Promised Land. Thus he died in the land of Moab, and they buried him in a valley of Moab, but his sepulcher remained unknown to the children of Israel. Moses was a hundred and twenty years old when he died, and the children of Israel wept for him in the plains of Moab for thirty days. Before his death he had laid his hands on Joshua, the son of Nun, and thus he too became a man who was full of the Spirit of wisdom. (see Deuteronomy 34)

It was then, according to the book of Joshua, chapter 1, that God made known to Joshua that he was to lead His people in to conquer the land.

1. THE COMMANDS TO TAKE THE LAND

> Go over this Jordan, you and all this people, unto the land which I do give to them. 2

Only be strong and very courageous that you may observe to do according to all the law, which Moses my servant commanded you. 7

Turn not from my law to the right hand or to the left, that you might prosper wherever you go. 7

This book of the law shall not depart out of your mouth, but you shall meditate therein day and night, so that you might observe to do according to all that is written therein. 8

Be strong and of good courage; be not afraid, neither be dismayed; for the Lord your God is with you, wherever you go. 9

2. THE PROMISES BACKING THE COMMANDS

I have given you every place your foot shall tread. 3

No man will be able to stand before you all the days
of your life. 5

I will be with you as I was with Moses. 5

I will not fail you nor forsake you. 5

3. THE WORDS OF ENCOURAGEMENT

Be strong and of good courage 6
for you shall divide the land
which I swore unto their fathers to give them
as an inheritance.

"Preacha," Dink jumped in, "don't ya tink dese people had ta be fearful as dey thought 'bout leavin' da wilderness ta go inta da Promised Land, as nice as that might sound?"

I told Dink I agreed that they must have had some reservations about doing what God commanded, just as we do, when God calls us to do His will with our lives! A call to some ministry? A call to go to a certain place to serve Him? A call to move from some familiar and safe place to a site of uncertainty in many ways? A call to do something for which we do not have the funds, or even the promise of the funds, but we must go completely by faith, trusting Him to supply our needs? A call to put even our children in His hands, as we go to some uncertain place? A call to face not just worldly men who might oppose us, but even more disheartening, to face professing believers, who give little evidence of being saved, as such people make up His church many times? A call to face people who say they believe the Word of God, but don't act like they do, as we seek to lead them in the way of the Lord?

A call to serve God will always have a positive joy about it, but we will soon find out that there are also negatives and questions we must face by faith. So it was that Joshua must have known the difficulty and problems of the task, as did the people.

Two things would immediately face them! And anyone who knew anything about the path, which stood before them, must have known of these immediate difficulties. There was the Jordan River. How were they to cross it? And there was the city of Jericho, which was a city of high walls and a warring people. How could they ever defeat them, when they could not get into the city to do battle?

But does not faith overcome all fear and doubt?

46 Does a Wrong Make a Right?

The next day was a rather uneventful one, as the biggest event was to take place that evening, when Ronnie Filmore was supposed to come through on his promise to supply us with our original set of the Sangster books. Dink called about 5:00 that evening and said that Ronnie wanted to meet us in the same parking lot at school, where he had found us the other day. He wanted to meet about 9:00 PM. Dink and I were there, and so was Ronnie right on time. He parked in a rather dark place, away from any bright lights on the campus.

"Ya gots da books?" Dink asked him, almost immediately.

"Yeah, I've got the books! But first things first!" he insisted.

"Well, what's does ya wants first den?" Dink asked suspiciously.

"I want yours and Dr. Pointer's promise of money for a plane ticket to Australia! Make it a business class seat, because I want to leave the good old USA forever in style! Plus, I'm going to trust you two with a promise for a ticket, because you are supposed to be preachers, and preachers are supposed to tell the truth!" he declared.

"How about da books?" Dink insisted again. "When does we gets even ta see dem, knowin' how sneaky you'se been in da past?"

"I will let you see them right now, and you can look them over, but the sale is not complete, which means you don't get the merchandise, until I have the money!" he informed us.

He went to the trunk of his car and opened it, where there was a number of boxes, which we supposed contained the books. He said he had no objection, if we wanted to browse through them, but we could not take any of them out of his sight! So we counted the books, and then went over each one of them carefully, writing down the titles, checking, their authenticity with Ronnie's flashlight, as best we could. They appeared to be genuine, yea, the very copies of the ones we had possessed previously, before they were stolen and supposedly destroyed. Then Dink asked him a another question.

"Does dis mean you ain't gonna testify in person at Clark Compton's trial?"

"Absolutely not! By the time of the trial, I will be long gone. I know too much for my own good. I need to get out of the country before I'm forced to testify against Compton, and even before I'm held accountable for my crimes!"

"So ya wants us ta bail ya outta yer years of crime by buyin' youse a ticket ta wherever it was! Ain't ya ever heard of aidin' and abettin' a criminal?"

"Yeah, but you boys haven't got a chance in court without these books! Compton will destroy you without this evidence. I probably could have set the price even higher, and you would have paid it. You don't have any other choice! Don't you know that your situation is hopeless without these books?"

"No, we's don't know dat! We knows dis---dat ya can't do right by doin' wrong! Yer right! We are in a bind! But it would never be right ta break da law, just ta get a leg up on old Clark. We knows dat! An' we knows dis! Our God is still on da throne! He's gonna determine da outcome of dis whole situation---fer us an' fer you. You'd do better by surrenderin' ta da Lord and gettin' saved dan by tryin' ta flee da country an' yer crimes!"

47 Faith or Obedience or Both?

We knew when we left Ronnie that we might never see him or the books again. He showed no interest in trusting the Lord, but that is surely the way of a lost man. He wold rather trust in himself and his own wits for the future, even when his world is falling in on him, than turn to the Lord. Such only proves the blindness of the human heart and the confidence of man in himself rather than in God, whatever the hour of his life. Whether we ever saw the books again, was completely in the hands of the Lord. He knew our need of them, as did we. But only He knew if and how we would ever get them again. He is able, if it is His will, was our confidence!

We decided that while we were already together there at my office, we would go in and look at the Word of God again before going home. We took up where we had left off previously in the first chapter of Joshua.

Following God's command to Joshua in the early part of our chapter, Joshua then spoke to the people themselves, giving them some very serious words for the future. He told the people to prepare food supplies, for within three days they would pass over the Jordan River to go in and possess the land, which God had given them.

The response of the children of Israel was that they would do all that the Lord had commanded them, and wherever Joshua sent them, they would go. As they had hearkened unto Moses in all things, so they would hearken to Joshua. They stated that they strongly desired for the Lord to be with Joshua, as He had been with Moses.

All of this initial challenge to go in and posses the land in obedience to the Lord was followed by a pledge from the people. They agreed that whosoever rebelled against

Joshua's commandment and would not hearken to his words in all that he commanded would be put to death!

We must remember that these are the people who had spent the last forty years wandering in the wilderness. Therefore, many of them remembered the results of the disobedience, which came to their older generation because of the lack of faith to obey the Lord in all that He commanded at Kadesh-barnea. Others had been born after the rebellion at Kadesh-barnea and had grown up listening to the sad stories of the unbelief of Israel. They had seen many die in the wilderness outside the blessing of the Promised land, which would have been theirs, had they walked in faith and obedience to their God!

Is it any wonder that they stood at this point of their lives and soberly and seriously stated:

1. We will do all that the Lord has commanded us!
2. We will go wherever Joshua sends us!
3. We will obey Joshua as we did Moses!
4. We want God to be with Joshua as He was with Moses!
5. We agree that all rebellion will be met with death!

About this time Dink jumped in, as usual, not capable of being silent and declared, "Preacha, dis is anudder of dose passages which stresses da seriousness of walking in faith and obedience to da Lord! I really wonders if many of God's professin' people taday realize dat dey ain't saved to make demselves happy doin' whats dey wants ta do? Don't dey know dat dey are bound an' obligated ta be servants ta God---ta go wheres He wants dem ta go; ta do what He wants dem ta do; ta be whats He wants dem ta be; ta say what He wants dem ta say; ta stay where He wants dem ta stay. We is His servants, and He is not our servant!

"An where would we as God's professin' people be if all rebellion was met wid death! Wow! Dat'd mean a lot of empty churches, cause how many church people der are dat tink da church belongs ta dem, an it exists ta please dem, an it can be run any way dey wants ta run it, wid little or no concern for da Word of God or da glory of God."

I jumped back in saying, "What a difference in God's people now compared to Kadesh-Barnea, when they at first refused to go, and then thought they could go up by themselves to take the land. At Kadesh-barnea it was at first a battle between God and the Canaanites, but then by their unbelief they made it a battle between themselves and the Canaanites, and they were miserably defeated, which is always the result when the battle is between us and the enemy. That's what was so important about our turning down Ronnie's offer---it was a way of the enemy to make it a battle between us and him instead of keeping it a battle between him and God.

"May we never forget that faith and obedience always make our lives a battle, not between us and the enemy, but between God and the enemy. Only a fool would want it otherwise, yet sometimes we are the fools, as we boldly but ignorantly battle the enemy, trusting in something else other than God and His power.

"As CHM says, 'The Lord's presence with His people secures victory over every foe, but if He be not with them, they are as water poured upon the ground.' We must always remember that grasshoppers (which we are without the Lord) are no match for giants! And if it is true as Jesus said, 'according to your faith, so be it unto you,' so it is also true 'that according to your unbelief, so be it unto you.'" (Mackintosh, *Genesis to Deuteronomy,* p. 515)

48 Can I Become A Christian Now?

I have to admit that I thought much about Ronnie Filmore the next few days. I hoped maybe he would change his mind and call us to let us know that he would give us the books without any strings attached. But it wasn't to be! He did call Dink and tell him he wanted to meet us again, and that he had another offer to make us concerning the books, but he never showed up, though we waited for him well past the designated hour. Finally, we went home, mulling over in our minds what this meant for Ronnie and us! When several days went by, and we still heard nothing, we figured the worst for Ronnie and for the books we had hoped to have, but not the worst for us, because our God was still in control of all things.

I did think and pray for Ronnie, wondering what had become of him, and if there was anything we could do to help him. Was he in the house, where he could live his days out till he died? Or was he in the pit, where they threw him directly without any tomfoolery, because he knew their plans anyway? But then I realized that we could never find the house or the pit again without the help of George Carlson, and who knew where he was or how to contact him? Thus we were back where we had started from with nothing to which we could cling, and nothing whereby we could be encouraged by human plans or human means. We were totally dependent on the Lord once again for the outcome of this situation. Not that He couldn't use human means, if He so desired, but that He didn't want our confidence to be in human means, but in Him.

Finally, five days later I got a phone call from Clark Compton himself. He spoke with guarded words and even with a sweet cordial attitude, which would have convinced anyone but us that he was a gracious and congenial man.

"Well, Dr. Pointer, I understand that we both have just suffered a great loss of a friend and some valuable materials, which we had hoped would be dealt with by another in a proper manner! Please, let me extend my condolences to you in this great loss! I do hope this doesn't inconvenience you in any great manner, and if I can be of further service to you concerning these issues we discussed or any other matter, please do not hesitate to get in touch with me. I meant what I said the other day about you and your friend joining our faculty. Maybe we can get together, after these other things are all settled, which I know we both hope is very soon. Yes, then we can talk about those teaching positions further. Thanks for everything, and I will be in touch!"

I called Dink and told him about it, and he took it all in stride! His remark was, "Preacha, der was a time in my life dat I'd a crushed dat guy fer such gross tactics, but now its all up ta da Lord! Old Clark's day's a comin', when all da world will know what he is! All in da Lord's time, no matter what he does now ta try ta stop it!"

As I thought on these matters, I was interrupted by another phone call. It is truly unique how the Lord works! This call was from Sam, the policeman, who had indicated that he would help us, for he had the same desire as Ronnie.

"Dr. Pointer?" he began the conversation.

When I replied in the affirmative, he opened his heart, which clearly was deeply troubled.

"Dr. Pointer! You've got to help me! Have you heard what happened to Ronnie Filmore?"

"Has something happened to him?" I asked, at least indicating that I knew him.

"He's been eliminated by Clark for something he did---I'm not sure what it was! But he's gone now---forever. That's the word around Clark's inner circle of hoods! They are saying that it's also a warning to anyone else who turns traitor!"

"So, why did you call me?" I asked him.

"Well, because I want out and I want out now---before the same thing happens to me!" he replied with a nervousness in his voice.

"I suggest then that you either leave the organization, and disappear to some place where they will never find you, or turn yourself over to the authorities---certainly not your police force there in Comptonville. That's your only two choices! When you've been a crooked cop, there aren't many places where you can hide!"

"I can't do any of those things! They're too dangerous! They'll find me wherever I go! They'll bring me back to Comptonville, regardless!" he argued.

"Well, then, it seems you have no other choices! Do you expect to live a life of sin with a constant breaking of the law of God and man, and at the end of it all, when you get tired of it, just to step out of that life into a fresh life? Do you expect things to be then just as if your past sin and wrongdoing had never taken place, or that all those years will just vanish away?" I argued.

"Please, help me!" he said, as his emotions broke.

"First, I am not sure you are on the level. You might be lying to me for Clark Compton and his purposes. Second, my dependence is not on men, neither you nor Compton, but upon the Lord. If you want to go to the police and let them protect you for your testimony against Clark Compton, then I suggest you get yourself a lawyer, and let him guide you as to the best route to take. Third, another way is possible, though every route has its dangers. You can keep playing ball with Clark, and at the right moment you can give your testimony against him. Please don't ask me to hide you or to help you. We've been through that before with someone else that you know [I didn't use Ronnie Filmore's name, but he knew who I meant], and it didn't work. There might be a fourth way, but it could be too dangerous too. You could find some of Compton's goons who are thinking like you, but the problem there is how to know who is loyal to him and who might not be. I am sure he has his spies in the midst of the ones who work for him, keeping their eyes on the store, while they might act like they are open to rebellion within the ranks!"

I felt sorry for him, and then I offered to do something for him, which Clark Compton couldn't stop. I told him I would pray for him, even now, that he would come to know Christ and His peace! He replied that was what his wife had been telling him for years---that his greatest need was the Lord and salvation.

It was there on the phone, after about another thirty minutes of explaining to him what a Christian was, that he prayed to be saved. Evidently, his Christian wife had planted the seed for years, and it had been watered also for a long duration, and I was privileged to see God give the increase. I was always hesitant to see a profession under such pressing circumstances, but then again, is this not the time when God does at times move upon the hearts of men? But at the same time, we must be careful in such a setting, lest a man wants the Lord only to help him out of his present troubles, and there is not a sincere repentance or understanding of what sin and salvation really are.

We closed our conversation with prayer, and he couldn't thank me enough for helping him in this hour!

49 Will There Be Faith at the Jordan?

Dink stopped by later in the day, and we discussed the event of the morning, that is, the profession of faith by Sam, the policeman. We were rejoicing over what God was doing, even in the midst of the most difficult of circumstances. Following this time of rejoicing, we turned to the Word of God once again, Joshua, chapter 2.

The context of this chapter is another sending out of men to spy out the land. But the difference seems to be that God initiated this as part of His providence, which was for His reasons. What reason, one might ask? Was it not because one of His own, that is, one of His elect, was in that city, and this was His means of saving her and the members of her family, before the city was destroyed? Rahab, as a Gentile, yet one of His elect, is a unique study, even within itself, but that was not our pursuit at this moment.

We mention the spies only to note God's use here of human means to accomplish His purposes, that is, the salvation of a woman and her family, even though the rest of the city would be destroyed. God has His ways and means, and they are not always the same in every instance. Two men were sent out at this time as spies to view the city of Jericho, the first city they would encounter upon entering the land after crossing the Jordan

As one reads this chapter carefully, something else is clear! The old attitude of rebellion is gone, and God's people are ready now to conquer the land. It is also clear that God continues to give them assurance of that fact, and they receive God's promises by faith---not from a heart of unbelief, like their forefathers at Kadesh-barnea. Years of wandering in the wilderness and seeing the previous generation die without receiving the promise, because of their rebellion, has prepared their hearts. Even hearing the story of Kadesh-barnea retold time and again, not only was used by God to build faith, but also to bring a fear that any future rebellion might also rob them of the privilege of entering and conquering the Promised Land.

The verses we have seen previously in chapter 1 show this attitude of faith very clearly, as there was a great respect for Joshua and his leadership and a pledge to obey the Lord and His servant. But now, even as the story in chapter two unfolds, the presence of the faith of God's people is confirmed. God's salvation of Rahab, though she was a harlot, and her willingness to help them, speaks of the providence and power of God! Rahab hiding the spies on her roof, and then sending them away, speaking words of faith in their God, surely did the same.

What were her words of faith? Listen to them, for they tell not only of her faith, but of the impact of the God of Israel upon the nations of the land, which they would enter:

> 9 I know that the Lord hath given you the land, and that your terror is fallen upon us, and that all the inhabitants of the land faint because of you. 10 For we have heard how the Lord dried up the water of the Red Sea for you, when you came out of Egypt, and what you did unto the two kings of the Amorites, who were on the other side of the Jordan, Sihon and Og, whom you utterly destroyed. 11 And as soon as we heard these things, our hearts did melt, neither did there remain any more courage in any man, because of you; for the Lord your God, he is God in heaven above, and in earth beneath.

Following these words, Rahab asked to be remembered, when they entered the land, and her request is granted---she and her family will be spared. She then let the men down by a cord through the window, and they fled to the mountains, until it was safe for them to return to the children of Israel on the other side of the Jordan. And what were the words of these spies when returning? Were they not far different from the spies sent out at Kadesh-barnea?

> 24 And they said to Joshua, Truly the Lord has delivered into our hands all the land; for even all the inhabitants of the country do faint because of us.

Thus they moved to the Jordan the next day, where they were given instructions for crossing it. There were no questions, no rebellions, nor doubting at this point of their journey---only a solemnity before the Lord, as they awaited His commands. They had learned the lessons of faith from the previous years of waiting in the wilderness.

Dink was bubbling by now, as usual, as he commented, "Preacha, don't dat teach us sometin'? When we'se compare da people of Israel now under Joshua wid da children of Israel as dey came outta Egypt, isn't da lessen clear? Dat faith is essential in servin' da Lord! And dat it takes time fer us to learn faith! Faith is kind of like a muscle of da body! Exercising it builds it up and makes it stronger. Dat's why God sends da trials, an' each time we is victorious in a trial, little faith gets stronger. Little faith may at times tink he can't bear the weight, but God gives strength, as little faith presses against the weight of da trial, an' he gets a little stronger. Den after years an' years of trials, little faith becomes slowly greater faith, and den greater faith becomes mighty faith! Amen, Brother Ira!"

50 Another Way to Get Clark Compton?

Several days passed, as we waited for further word on matters, especially concerning whether the court would consider again the issue of who had the rights to manage Turnover News Agency. The only way Clark Compton could be defeated was to expose his motive for seeking to control and even destroy TNA---the motive being to cover up his plagiarism of the Sangster books. But to do that, obviously, we needed the books, which we no longer possessed. Mac had protested vigorously the takeover by Clark Compton, and he had pursued every legal possibility available without the books. But because of Clark's ties to so many of the big money men and the influential people of the world, it was an uphill battle, which never got off the ground. And his efforts may have convinced some that Mac was out to get Clark Compton, a good man. who was acting within the law, but was being persecuted by Mac Turnover, a bitter man with an ulterior motive.

Then the days turned into weeks as we waited, and all the while Turnover News Agency was growing weaker, as it was being strangled by Clark's efforts to bring everything to a halt before any further trial. Perhaps he hoped that the legal delay eventually would force us to negotiate a lopsided compromise, which would be, if he had his way, a total destruction of us and Mac and TNA. What did he care if Mac and TNA died, or if we were destroyed also?

Then as I was meditating and praying on this matter, I received a call from Dr. Graham. He expressed sympathy for us and the situation, and then he made a suggestion.

"Since we are not getting anywhere in the courts, I would like to ask yours and Dink's and Mac's permission to take this to the board of trustees of Clark Compton's seminary!" he suggested.

I chuckled over the phone, as I knew the difficulty of a person or a group of persons asking an independent seminary board to do something. During the time of the recent inerrancy battle, our denomination in its annual national meeting had voted to ask the trustees of each seminary to bring their individual school back in line with the historic Baptist doctrine of Scripture. I wrote them (every one of the trustees of every seminary) urging them to be open and sensitive to the desire of the vote of the annual convention. But they did nothing about the problem, except that two out of the dozens of trustees I had written, wrote back to me, telling me they would do as they pleased, regardless of what the denomination said or desired! I shared that with Dr. Graham, and told him I appreciated his suggestion, but I really didn't think it would get very far.

He replied, "Yes, I know all about that issue, and the way the seminaries are governed by trustees."

I felt badly, and so I apologized for my thoughtless statement. I hoped he didn't think I was trying to lecture him on the governing of a seminary. After all, he was the president of one, and he surely knew more about those kinds of matters than I did. Perhaps, he did have a plan on how to face our problem through the seminary where Clark Compton served as president.

"No," he insisted, "don't take my statement as any rebuke. Just listen and give me your feedback on my idea!"

I was open to hear what he said, as I realized that when you are backed into a corner, like we were, who knows what the answer might be, and who might suggest it! Surely, I should be wise enough to listen to someone with more experience than I have had in the affairs and politics of seminary life, especially at a time like this! His plan was simple, and after he shared it with me, and we had discussed it for awhile, I was convinced it very well might be the Lord's answer to our problem.

Dr. Graham's idea was that he would go to the other presidents of our denomination's seminaries, and present them with the Clark Compton situation, its seriousness, along with the evidence. We would hope that he could persuade these presidents to at least agree to talk with the Chairman of the Executive Committee of the Board of Clark Compton's seminary, showing him the evidence, also, and its seriousness. If we could convince the Chairman of Clark Compton's Executive Committee, then he could take it to the entire Board of Trustees of that school, and let them deal with it by examining the evidence and deciding what to do with it.

My reply was more of a thought than an objection.

"That is a lot of people to convince, which could take a lot of time, which might give a lot of opportunities for a lot of leaks, which might expose what we are doing before we could explain fully the evidence and its seriousness. Which also means that Clark Compton might jump in at any time to set up his defense and convince many of those minds that he was innocent of all the charges, as well as allow him to turn loose his guns upon us."

"Let him do it!" Dr. Graham said forcefully with conviction. "Let him expose it to the whole world, and that really will set off an investigation by someone---other news agencies, etc."

I sat there in my chair hanging on to the phone, amazed over the boldness of Dr. Graham---my kind of man!

51 Was There Faith at Jericho?

As Dink and I had been waiting for some word concerning a court date, we didn't see much of each other. We were both spending as much time with our families as possible, because we didn't know where a trial would be or how long it would take us away from home. But with Dr. Graham's new plan, some amazing and almost unbelievable things began to take place, which evidenced we might soon be facing Clark Compton before his trustees. Dr. Graham's meeting with the seminary presidents went well, and they were in agreement with the plan. Then, as these seminary presidents all met with Dr. Madison, the Chairman of the Executive Board of Clark Compton's seminary, he seemed opposed, until he saw the agreement of his peers and Dr. Graham's strong conviction. Dr. Graham assured him that Dink and I and Mac were not some kind of agitators or nuts, who were just after Compton, but that some clear evidence actually backed our claims. But the most amazing thing was that all of this took place within a week's time, which surely must have been in our favor, as it seemed to keep the word of our plan from getting back to Clark Compton himself. Yes, as amazing as it was, we were to be engaged in battle with Clark Compton before his full board of trustees that next week!

It was then that I called Dink and suggested that we encourage our hearts by renewing our study of God's people, as they faced the impossible task of conquering Jericho! Surely there was something we could learn from this passage!

It is reported in the Bible in Joshua 6 that Jericho was securely shut up because of the children of Israel. No one went in and no one went out. In simple words the gates were securely closed, so that Israel could not go in the gates. But the city was also strong walled, even two sets of walls, and the walls were so thick, that it is reported that they could conduct chariot races on those walls. There was no way through the gates! There was no way over the walls! An army, it seems, could be slaughtered seeking to scale two sets of walls, and there was no way through the walls, because they were too thick. And there was no way under the walls! All of this surely presented to Joshua and the children of Israel an impossible situation.

All the children of Israel possessed at this moment was God's command to take the city, and God's directions concerning how to do it, and God's promise that He would give them the city. And as one reads this chapter, if he was still thinking of the unbelief of Israel at Kadesh-barnea, prior to the wandering in the wilderness, one might expect another of Israel's moments of hesitancy and unbelief in light of the impossibility of the task before them. Note carefully the Lord's words to His people at this moment:

GOD'S PROMISE

> 2 See, I have given into thine hand Jericho, and its king, and the mighty men of valor.

GOD'S DIRECTIONS

> 3 And you shall compass the city, all you men of war, and go round about the city once. Thus you shall do six days. 4 And seven priests shall bear before the ark seven trumpets of rams' horns; and the seventh day you shall compass the city seven times, and the priests shall blow with the trumpets. 5 And it shall come to pass that, when they make a

> long blast with the ram's horn, and when you hear the sound of the trumpet, all the people shall shout with a great shout; and the wall of the city shall fall down flat, and the people shall ascend up, every man strait before him. 10 And Joshua had commanded the people, saying, You shall not shout, nor make any noise with your voice, neither shall any word proceed out of your mouth, until the day I bid you shout; then shall you shout.

I sat in amazement as I read this story! There is not one word of disagreement or disobedience. I read the story expecting someone to disavow the plan or the leader for his simplicity to follow such a plan! Walk around the city six days one time each day for six days, not making one sound ---period. No sound of the voice, no shouting as they walked around the city, not one word coming from their mouths, till Joshua gave the word on the seventh day, after they had walked around the city seven times on that seventh day. Then they were to shout!

Would not the carnal mind of unbelief find much to criticize here? What kind of plan is this? What will it hurt to talk to each other as we walk? What good will it do to walk around the city? Why one time for seven days? Why seven times on the seventh day? What will the Jerichoites think we are doing? Won't they laugh at us? Will they not think we are mad? Will they not know what we are doing is silly and impossible, as far as conquering the city? What if we do all of that and then shout as Joshua says, and nothing happens? What then? And you tell me that Joshua is a military man? Where did he get a plan like that? What does Joshua think our shouting is going to do to Jericho? Scare them to death? More likely they will be rolling on the ground holding their sides while they laugh at us! This is silly! I'm not going! Let's go back over the Jordan River! We can settle there. Let's elect a new leader if we have to, in light of Joshua's delusion to think that he alone is able to know God's will and lead God's people!

Not one such word---nothing but obedience and faith in the face of an impossible situation, where they had God's command, God's promise, and God's power by faith, as they were obedient to Him and followed His directions.

Again, Dink couldn't wait until I was finished.

"Wow, Preacha, dats where we is right now---waitin' fer da big battle. No evidence, which we can use ta defend ourselves! No witnesses, dat carry much weight! No goons ta carry our water fer us in dis dry desert of falsehood! All evidence, as far as we knows, is destroyed! No high-priced lawyer ta twist da truth! Only a few seminary presidents who have gotten da door open fer us, but now God must give da victory. Are we'se defeated? No more dan da childrens of Israel! Fer our hope is not in men nor in men's power, but in da Lord! God's never failed us before, an' He ain't gonna fail us now before da entire board!"

We prayed and committed the matter to the Lord once again, and as we ended, we were greeted by a phone call.

"This is George Carlson! I hope you are encouraged tonight! God will come through for us. He never fails! I like the new plan! There will be some surprises before this is over! But God will prevail! Sorry, I have been out of touch. I'll be there tomorrow!" he said, and then hung up.

Jokingly, I thought to myself, "I hope he brings a set of the Sangster books with him!"

52 Where Is the Evidence?

Monday morning of the next week found us on a plane heading to the city where we would finally get our day (or days---who knew then how long it might take) before the whole board of Mid-City Baptist Seminary. Present, too, would be Clark Compton and his goons. He by now had been informed of the meeting, and who knew what he might have planned to stop or disrupt the meeting.

We were met at the airport by Dr. Graham, who had flown up on Sunday afternoon to meet with the seminary presidents, including Dr. Madison, the Chairman of the Board of Trustees of Mid-City Baptist Seminary. Dr. Graham checked all the details of the proceedings, just so we would have everything covered, so there would be no surprises. The meetings were to be similar to a courtroom, but more of a hearing, where there would be testimony and then opportunity for cross-examination and rebuttal of evidence presented. Each side could have a lawyer to represent them. There would be an impartial judge to hear and govern the case, but the final determination, and any recommendation of the need to file further charges would be made by the Mid-City Baptist Seminary Board of Trustees, not just the Executive Board, as we had hoped. One other problem---where was George Carlson?

I must confess that Compton's trustees having the final word on the matter gave me some concern. At worst, how many of these trustees were handpicked (over the years of course), as Clark Compton cronies? Or at best, how many were just loyal gullible friends of his, who would not believe the evidence, as strong as it might be?

We arrived at the seminary and were escorted into the seminary boardroom by none other than Clark Compton's security men (goons). That did not make me feel too comfortable, as a couple of them were those who had taken us to the death house! When all were seated, the judge entered and called the group to order. He began to tell us procedures and rules that were to be followed in this hearing. It was during this time that a man from the crowd walked up to our lawyer. There was something familiar about him, but I couldn't figure out what. After a few words with our lawyer, he returned to his seat.

When the judge was finished, and it was our turn to present the evidence against Clark Compton first, I was shocked when the first one called to the stand was George Carlson! George Carlson? Was he in the room? Then as I looked around, I saw the man who had just spoken to our lawyer coming down the aisle---the man I thought I recognized. As he stepped forward to take the witness stand, he removed a wig and other portions of a disguise. The primary lawyer of Clark Compton's legal beagles objected, because that name was not on his list of expected witnesses. Our lawyer explained that he had just found out about George Carlson's presence in the room, and he would make all the difference in this case! The judge ruled his witness was acceptable, as we were not a normal courtroom that had to follow all the strict rules of procedure.

As George took the stand, our lawyer gave him free reign to tell his whole story: who he was; how he had grown up in Comptonville with Clark Compton; how his father had been a deacon at the First Baptist church and a close friend to William Sangster; the whole story of William Sangster; what Clark and his father had done to William Sangster and his writings; and how Clark Compton had plagiarized them and then ridden them to a college teaching position---even to the presidency of a seminary.

Clark Compton was about to have a conniption fit, as he squirmed in his chair, while his lawyer tried to calm him. This was a rare time in his life, when he could not control the events going on around him! And he didn't like it!

When George was finished, Clark Compton's lawyer was allowed to cross-examine him. His first question was, did he have any evidence to back up all those ridiculous claims? Did he have the books, which he claimed had been written by this William Sangster, which Clark Compton was supposed to have plagiarized? Did he have any evidence that there ever was a William Sangster, who had pastored the First Baptist Church of Comptonville?

George's answer was a calm admission that all the evidence that William Sangster had ever existed had been very carefully destroyed by the Compton family! All the evidence at the First Baptist Church of Comptonville was gone; all the evidence in the city of Comptonville, including the library, the newspaper office, and even in the cemetery, could not be found; all the evidence at the local Baptist associational office, and even the evidence that just a few weeks ago could have been found at the state Baptist office was now gone. He admitted that he had no evidence that William Sangster had ever existed, except for his witness and the witness of others and some of Dr. Sangster's remaining relatives. George also explained that he had possessed a set of the books, but they had been stolen and were supposed to have been destroyed by Clark Compton's men.

Of course, in bringing these confessions of no evidence from George, the Compton lawyer turned the tables on him and his testimony in order to destroy completely his credibility. The accusation became that his testimony was false, based on self-serving motives, so that he could destroy Clark Compton and his illustrious family.

You could sense the crowd's emotional shift from the shock they had experienced initially from George's testimony against Clark Compton. That shock had raised sincere doubts in their minds about Compton. But now a sympathy began to build for Clark Compton, and a strong disdain for George Carlson mounted in their minds. How and why did he bring such charges that could not be proven! Thus George Carlson left the witness stand viewed as an eccentric old man, who was making charges, which he could not substantiate.

Our lawyer then called on me to take the stand, and I must confess, it was not easy to follow George's testimony and the destruction of his claims, though they were true. I was asked by our lawyer to tell my story, which I did. I told of the student who came to me wishing to write on the life and ministry of his great-great-grandfather, William Sangster, and he even had a book written by him to show me! He told me of his father telling him the story of William Sangster! I informed them how Dink and I had gone to Comptonville, and how we were treated by the police! They told us to leave the library, then to leave the church, when we went there, and then they told us to get out of town! I told them that later we even went to talk to Clark Compton at Mid-City Baptist Seminary in his office! But then we were kidnapped and taken to a house in the mountains and given two choices! We could stay there at the house and die, or we could try to leave the house and die, trying to get back to civilization! We tried to escape, but we fell into a pit, and were in that pit for several days before George Carlson rescued us from the pit. He gave us a set of the Sangster books, and helped us escape and return home! But we were kidnapped again by Compton's men, only this time it was from Seminary City! We were taken to Comptonville, and put in jail there to await a trial for our supposed crimes in Comptonville! The bogus charges were finally dropped and we were released! Then the Sangster books were stolen from us, and that is the reason we do not have them as evidence today! Finally, we related how Clark Compton had bought stock in Turnover News Agency, so he could be an equal partner---all so he could stop Mac Turnover from exposing him as a fraud, a plagiarizer, a murderer, and a liar for those many years!.

As I was telling the story, I began to sense how impossible this all really sounded! I also began to see how Clark Compton's lawyer would seek to destroy my testimony also, when he cross-examined me! He surely would ask, "Do you really expect this crowd to believe such a fictitious tale of distress?" I could also tell that the crowd was more suspicious now, after having been swayed at first by George's testimony, only to find out that he had no evidence.

When I was finished, I braced myself for the moment of cross-examination. Sure enough, the Compton lawyer asked for evidence, of which I had to admit I had none. But my explanation of the reason why we had no evidence didn't seem to make any difference. I could have asked for them to question Clark Compton's goons, some of whom were in the room, but what good would that do? They would just deny it. And so I was dismissed, being called by Compton's lawyer nothing more than a man with a vivid imagination, and a history of problems with various authorities. The lawyer had researched some of my previous scrapes with authorities, which scrapes actually were no fault of my own. These came as I was seeking to help others, and he forgot to add that I was always exonerated of all false accusations. But though our lawyer sought to make that point, it seemed to be lost in the face of the charges we had made without any evidence and the ability of Compton's lawyer to poke fun at us.

Dink was the next one called to the stand, and he told the same story I had given, which should have substantiated my testimony. But, he, too, was scorched by the Compton lawyer as a flunky to me. After all, just consider Dink's history as a gang member of the Almandine! Then there were the years he was under my influence. Plus, there was the trauma of his own son being kidnapped not long ago (Belcher, *A Journey in Providence*), to say nothing of his supposed inability to speak the English language correctly.

It was the same with every witness we called---my student, William Sangster, and his father, and even character witnesses for both Dink and me. All were dismissed as cronies of sorts for us, possessing no evidence in the case. Even Mac Turnover was assaulted verbally. All of us were dismissed by the Compton lawyer as some kind of kooks (that is not the word he used, but that is what he meant), and Mac Turnover was just a man who couldn't get over a legitimate business deal whereby he had lost control of TNA. The lack of evidence became the bottom line of our whole case---evidence we had possessed, but which had been destroyed by Clark Compton!

Our testimony was followed by numerous character witnesses for Clark Compton. It may have been that many of them were very sincere in speaking such glowing words, and that they just knew him from afar and not as the man we had come to know. His backers were the cream of the crop of the rich and powerful and the influential people of the nation. By the time they and Compton's lawyer were finished, I am sure that many wondered why there was ever such a hearing to begin with! And why waste any more time in such fruitless efforts!

The session adjourned about 5:00 that afternoon, but the judge insisted that we would meet one more time to hear a suggested resolution of the findings of this gathering. The resolution would be drawn up by the other seminary presidents during our break, and would be presented to the Mid-City Baptist Seminary Board of Trustees for their consideration and final action. The judge apologized for asking everyone to have to stay through for an evening meeting, but he said it was necessary. He even mentioned that such a meeting may not have been necessary, but it was good to clear up these matters. How's that for a "homer" for a judge!

The Compton lawyer objected to another meeting, saying enough had been said to show any case against Clark Compton was absolutely and ridiculously bogus. Why, then, another meeting? In a sense I had to admit that he was right! Our testimonies had been totally dismissed, because of the lack of evidence, they said. It seems our witnesses were not considered as legitimate witnesses, and I wondered, why not? Was it just because we did not have the rich and powerful behind us? Maybe there was no reason to meet this evening. Just kill the case, get it over, and let the chips fall where they may. But then, I reminded myself, those were thoughts of unbelief.

But how could the case ever turn in our favor without evidence? And who had the time between 5:00 PM and 7:00 PM to go out and dig up some evidence, when we had been looking for such for months, but every piece of evidence had been destroyed by Clark Compton and his men. If I thought we had been painted into a corner before, and we had, I concluded there never had been such an impossible corner as this one!

As I watched the crowd leave the boardroom, I looked for George Carlson, but he was nowhere to be found. I seriously wondered, if he would be back that evening! I didn't see Dr. Graham, either. I wondered if he would be back! I noticed Clark Compton and his lawyer slapping each other on the back, as they were all smiles over the past meeting and full of confidence for the next. Finally, there was just Dink and Mac and I left sitting in the room, after the crowd cleared out. Our heads were buried in our hands! No one had spoken to us, either to encourage or to vilify us! As Dink and I sat in silence, I also went over our testimony in my mind, wondering what more we might have said or done to turn the case.

Things seemed more hopeless than any time previously in this whole ordeal. And now it was all going to end this evening, so it seemed. The walls around our Jericho were strong and thick and high. There was no way we could see to get over, through, or under these walls either. The enemy definitely seemed to have the upper hand.

I turned, as I heard Dink humming a tune, and then he looked and smiled at me. And, since the boardroom was empty, he began to sing softly, and soon I joined in.

Faith, mighty faith, the promise sees,
And looks to God alone.
Laughs at impossibilities,
And cries it shall be done
And cries it shall, it shall be done,
And cries it shall, it shall be done!
Laughs at impossibilities,
And cries it shall be done!

53 Could We Lose But Yet Win?

Dink and I didn't feel like eating any supper between the afternoon and evening sessions, so we went to our room and stretched out on the beds to rest and pray and talk, and I began the conversation.

"Dink, do you remember where we were in the book of Joshua, as the children of Israel stood before Jericho, and the impossibility of the task?"

"Sure do, Preacha, an' aint dat where we is taday?"

"What hope did they have---except the Lord!"

I went on to point out the impossibility of the task before them. Nothing had happened after they had walked around the city for six days---one time a day! But there still was no murmuring or complaining! Even when they began walking on the seventh day---no murmuring. Yet they did not walk around Jericho one time that day, but seven times!

I pointed out to Dink that this was the most difficult time, for if nothing happened that seventh day on the seventh time around the city, when they blew the trumpets and shouted, what would they do then? What will we do tonight, if the Lord doesn't come through? Will we not be totally discredited? Will not our reputations be ruined? Will not Dr. Graham probably be fired from his position for suggesting such a meeting? Will we not be relieved of our jobs at the seminary? And who knows what else could follow in the wake of such events for years to come!

Dink agreed that these things could and would probably all happen---if God failed to come through for us! Or could it be that God might get greater glory somehow out of what seemed to be a failure to us? Could He not bring victory out of seeming failure?

In our discussion we suggested that what appeared to be the greatest failure of history, turned out to be the greatest blessing and victory of all time! The seeming failure was the death of Christ! The greatest victory in history was His resurrection, which came from that seeming failure, and which Paul said was essential for the truth of the gospel. If Christ has not risen from the dead, then we are of all men most miserable! But He had to die before He could rise from the dead. Thus both death and resurrection were essential for the power of the gospel message for us.

Then the question became, which will it be tonight? Will it be victory through seeming failure or victory through the defeat of the enemy tonight? How the first (seeming failure) would come about was easy to see---we had seen the foundation of death being laid for us for many months, including today. But how the second (victory) would come about was beyond us to see---we saw no way out of this impossible corner in which God has placed us!

And there were other questions, which went through my mind. Would all the members of the board of trustees of Compton's seminary be back tonight? Some had come a great distance to be there for the meeting that day, and if they thought that they had seen enough in the afternoon session, had they already started home? Would Clark Compton even come back tonight, thinking the case was an easy victory for him? Would new evidence be allowed, even if some became available, or was this just a time for the vultures to circle the dead meat (us) and devour it?

Dink then noted, "Preacha, I's been in some tight places, when I was in da gang world, but none of dem compares wid dis one tonight! I could always do sometin' ta try ta change tings! But dis is all in da hands of da Lord! May His will be done, whatever it is!"

54 How Will This All End?

We drug ourselves from the comfort of those few moments, and then made our way back to the seminary to see what God was going to do. All was in His hands! The crowd didn't seem to have diminished, and I was sure that all were waiting for a decision in Clark Compton's favor, and that most thought it wouldn't be long in coming from the judge and then from the trustees.

Dr. Graham came by and whispered in my ear, "I hate to tell you this, but the presidents met during the break and prepared a resolution to be presented at the proper time tonight, exonerating Clark Compton of all accusations against him! I guess they are eager to get it over and go home!"

I shook my head, as I thought, they wouldn't even wait for the hearing to finish! What hope do we have, whatever might take place tonight?

Then the judge came in, took his seat, and struck his gavel to call the meeting to order. He was just about ready to read the statement from the seminary presidents, when George Carlson rose, and asked if he could address the meeting one more time! It was obvious that such a request did not please either the judge or the crowd, as some moaned, while the judge's face gave away his impatience as well. He must have thought, "What can this old man, who may be even a little bit senile, add to our meeting again, when he struck out so badly earlier today?" I had to confess his performance in the afternoon was a little lethargic and listless.

Then very graciously and quietly George said, "Please, Judge! I guarantee you won't be sorry. I now have the evidence to prove our case against Clark Compton!"

All must have wondered, and I must say, I had my concerns, if this was just an old man's last gasp to try to revive a hopeless situation. And I am sure that the trustees must have concluded that in light of their two families having clashed openly through the years, maybe George just wanted one more chance before the limelight to try to discredit Clark Compton, but without any evidence. A groan went up again, when the judge gave him permission to speak, but the judge warned him that if there was no evidence shown within a few minutes, he would be silenced, so the hearing could continue with its business.

With that permission George Carlson came slowly to the front of the boardroom and addressed the judge and asked if he could bring in his evidence. The judge seemed puzzled, and even further tempted to rule against him. But nonetheless, he shrugged his shoulders and gave agreement, thinking perhaps when such evidence was not forthcoming, that would be the end of the old man and his desire to have center stage. But much to his and our surprise, both doors swung open wide, and men began to invade the place, carrying boxes, and George Carlson came alive also, as they entered the room.

"Judge, and honored members of the Mid-City Baptist Seminary Board of Trustees!" he said with enthusiasm and vigor, almost with the staccato of a fiery preacher. "You asked for evidence, and I am giving you the evidence---now! These are boxes of books, which were written by Dr. William Sangster, formerly the pastor of the First Baptist Church of Comptonville. These are the books, which Clark Compton plagiarized to write his set of commentaries. These are the book he has tried so hard to destroy! There will be coming a second group of men carrying the Compton books into this court room, and I do challenge you to compare them, and then there will be no doubt in anyone's mind that all of the charges we have made against Clark Compton today are true! Clark Compton plagiarized all the works of Dr. William Sangster, and then sought to destroy all evidence of his crime, just as you have heard from these honorable men today."

As he spoke these words, more boxes of books were carried into the courtroom---further evidence of plagiarism from the hands of Clark Compton.

Then a large screen came down out of the ceiling, and an overhead projector was set up, and it was obvious George was getting ready to show the crowd a comparison of the two sets of books. As the lights faded into darkness, and the projector light beamed, George put up picture after picture of side by side comparisons of portions from the various books! And when he was finished, it could not be denied that someone had plagiarized someone! And it was not William Sangster who plagiarized Clark Compton!

As the lights came on, Clark Compton's lawyer was almost tying Compton down and clamping his hand over Compton's mouth to keep him for exploding publicly. His lawyer wanted to speak, but George beat him to the punch.

"Judge, I suggest that we take a recess, so that any and all board members who want to do so can come and compare any of these books, just to further satisfy the court that we have spoken the truth, proving our case!"

Compton's lawyer blurted out, "And I want to be the first to see these books and the comparisons!"

As they were all looking at the books, George turned and winked at us, and held up his index finger. I remembered his statement that there would be some surprises in the proceedings tomorrow, and I took that sign to mean the books were surprise number one.

Compton's lawyer tried a few tricks when the examination of the books was finished, such as suggesting the Sangster books were forgeries, and someone had printed them in that older looking form, as they were really forgeries of Clark Compton's work. But George Carlson was ready for that objection. Several men came in, and he introduced them as experts in the study of the age of various documents. He then presented letters from these men, showing the strength of their credentials, and then their conclusions concerning the age of both sets of books. Their conclusion was that, if anyone plagiarized anyone, it was Clark Compton who plagiarized William Sangster. Suddenly, the courtroom was open to hear further evidence, and George obliged them, as he took the floor once again.

"Your honor, the charge of plagiarism is not the only matter before us today. I would like to say something about the matter of Clark Compton's attempted takeover of Turnover News Agency."

Compton's lawyer quickly jumped to his feet to object!

"Your honor, there were no laws broken in the so-called takeover of the Turnover News Agency! It was a purely legitimate transaction, which happens every day in the world of buying and selling of stocks. There is absolutely no way anyone can overturn the purchase of the 50% of the stock of Turnover News Agency by Clark Compton!"

George was quickly on the offensive as he stated, "Oh, your honor, I didn't say it was an illegal action. I just said I would like to say something about that subject! I have some new light and evidence which I think I can clear up that subject, and I would like to present it here and now!"

Now the judge himself was confused.

"Well, if it was not illegal, what does it have to do with any charge you want to bring against Clark Compton?" he asked with a puzzled look on his face.

"Oh, again, Judge, I did not say I would like to bring any further charges against Clark Compton. I just want to inform you, and Clark Compton and his lawyer, and every other person in this room concerning a very important matter regarding the matter of Turnover News Agency. And I will, if you all will quit interrupting me!" he said with something of a humble rebuke in his voice. The room turned as quiet as a morgue in the middle of the night, as all were confused, and then George continued.

"I can prove that Clark Compton is not the sole heir of the Compton fortune, which means that all of his possessions, that he thinks are his, including TNA stock, must be equally divided with someone else, who is not in favor of what he has done concerning that news agency!"

Following this statement, the courtroom was overcome by all kinds of expressions, which could be heard audibly for a few moments, until the judge gaveled the court back to order. There were "ohs" and "ahs" and "groans" and "moans" and all kinds of other sounds, which expressed a wave of audible unbelief and further confusion. Even the judge let slip the words "You've got to be kidding!"

But the best expression to be found was that on the face of Clark Compton himself! The furthest thought on his mind, when he entered that room, was a statement of this sort. He had not only expected to win and settle this matter once and for all and return to his peaceful life as a seminary president, but to totally defeat and destroy those who had brought the accusations against him. And now he was about to see our claim of plagiarism against him fully vindicated, while something else was added to the mix of surprises also---the claim he was about to lose half of his fortune! No wonder his face was flushed and pale, and he looked like a man on his deathbed!

Our lawyer then walked to the judge's bench and presented a copy of something to the judge, at which time the judge called both lawyers together, and the Compton lawyer could only stand there reading and rereading and staring at the document, seemingly unable to believe what it said. Then other papers were presented, and the same routine was followed at the bench, as the judge and the lawyers conferred quietly, not saying a word out loud now. Every once in awhile, our lawyer would point out something to the judge, and the judge would in turn point it out to the Compton lawyer, and his only response was the puzzled action of the shaking of his head in unbelief.

In the meantime George Carlson sat in his chair as content as I have ever seen him! A smile came back over his face, but it was not the smile of a simpleton---it was the smile of victory! It was clear now, that all through the events of the day, he had possessed this information. But he had toyed with the court, waiting to present it at this climactic moment for sake of effect on the hearts and minds of all who were present---especially the mind and heart of Clark Compton!

The only question left now was, "What is on that sheet of paper?"

55 Look What God Did!!

It seemed like time had stopped, or that it was surely crawling, as the crowd waited for the report of the information, which was on that one piece of paper, which had brought this court session to an instant halt. The Compton lawyer, which number quickly became lawyers, couldn't look at the paper enough times to satisfy themselves. Over and over their eyes scanned it, whatever it was, as if they were looking for some way out of what it said---some argument, some loophole, some mistake, some question that could be raised. Our train was back on the track, and it seemed now that they could not stop it! But, again, what did that paper or document say?

Finally, the judge called for a brief recess with the explanation that the court needed to make a phone call to check some information, which had come to light! He and the lawyers left the boardroom, and that led to all kinds of speculation, as the place buzzed with guesses and questions. In the meantime, George Carlson, the only man left in the court room, who knew the contents of the document which he had presented, sat looking like the cat who had just swallowed the canary---all smiles and perfect contentment. No wonder he appeared so satisfied---he had been waiting for this moment for years!

Clark Compton seemed beside himself, and he had tried to flag down his lawyer, so he could find out what was on that piece of paper, but the judge had stopped him, until he could make his check of the information. So all Clark could do was sit and look like the cat, which had tried to swallow a turkey! He was miserable, impatient, and understandably so, because here was a situation over which he had no control. He hadn't faced such moments very often in his life previously, and he did not like it now!

Finally, they all returned to the room, and the judge called the group back into session. After clearing his throat several times, he still seemed reluctant to do so, but he made the following announcement:

> The court has just received documented information that the same man fathered both George Carlson and Clark Compton, which makes them half brothers. That means that George Carlson is an heir to the Compton fortune, and that he owns half of the entire Compton holdings and properties and finances in the Compton complex of businesses and possessions, as it now exists Not only the holdings and possessions which existed at the time of their father's death, but all holdings and possessions, which will have accumulated at the time of the disclosure of this information of joint heirs. That means also (and we have checked and re-checked with the original lawyers who drew up the document) that George Carlson owns 25% of the stock in the Turnover News Agency, as does Clark Compton. Which means, also, that neither Clark Compton nor George Carlson can stalemate TNA, unless they both agree to act together, which we will leave them to decide.
>
> In my contact with the law firm, which handled the will and estate of the father of these two men, they have affirmed that this is a legal and proper document, which was drawn up by the elder Mr. Compton. He knew that George Carlson was his son, and he wanted after his death, to do that which was

right towards him, for the grief he and his family have suffered through the years.

It is my understanding that this document has been in the possession of George Carlson, since his father died, and he could have used this document to claim his inheritance any time during his life, in accordance with his wishes. I therefore, as the appointed judge of this hearing, declare two things: 1) that Clark Compton plagiarized the works of Dr. William Sangster, and 2) that he is also obligated to turn over half of his holdings and possessions to George Carlson, which includes half of his stock in Turnover News Agency.

Realize that this hearing is not the final word on this matter, as we can only declare our findings as our convictions. Legal courts will have to bring the final declaration. And the Board of Trustees of Mid-City Baptist Seminary will also have to decide the future of Clark Compton in relation to their institution.

A strike of the gavel was followed by an uproar from the crowd! Some, I am confident, were rejoicing like Dink and I were, and others were moaning with Clark Compton over the unexpected turn of events. Mac soon found us, and we were all hugging and rejoicing! Now Mac was free to write his story exposing Clark Compton for what he really was---a plagiarizing, lying, pretender, who did not deserve to be the president of the seminary, and neither could he take over the news agency as he so desired.

I made my way over to George Carlson, but before I could say anything, he said, "I told you I would be there when you needed me, and that there would be some surprises in the courtroom today. God's day of retribution has come, and I must say, His righteousness being upheld in behalf of us, His servants, is a very satisfying thing!"

I couldn't help but ask him, even though the noise in the court room was still deafening, how long he had known he was Clark Compton's half brother?

He replied, "My father, the man who raised me as his son, though he was not my biological father, told me years ago, when I was in my early twenties. He finally showed me the legal papers some years later, when he was on his deathbed. But he asked me to promise him that I would not use that information as long as the elder Mr. Compton was still alive. Nor was I to use it just to become a rich man. My father was a very wise individual, and he was broken-hearted to see Clark Compton beginning to use Dr. Sangster's labor for his own benefit. Though he couldn't have dreamed how far Clark Compton would go in smearing and destroying the entire memory of Dr. Sangster, my father suspected the day would come when he would do something of this nature.

"Thus I waited until the right moment so that the fall of Clark Compton would be the lowest and most humbling moment of his life---just when he thought he had the world by the tail, and that no one could stop him. Yes, at the epitome of his success and arrogance and confidence, we pulled the rug out from under him. He will surely spend the rest of his life in jail in light of all these other cans of worms, which have been opened tonight, as they are pursued to their proper ends. And his tenure as a seminary professor or teacher or denominational big shot is over! The one who was praised so much for such brilliance of mind and skill in writing commentaries has now been shown to be the fraud that he has been all his life. And though I feel sorry for him, I weep no tears for him. As the old saying goes, he has made his bed and he must now lie in it. The way of the transgressor is surely hard!"

"But where did the books come from?" I asked again. "Weren't they destroyed? Was there another set of the Sangster books, or did you find the stolen ones?"

He turned and pointed to Sam in the audience, who was hugging his wife and crying.

"Sam found them yesterday, and he got them to me early this morning!" he admitted.

"You had them during the morning sessions, and didn't use them then?" I asked in unbelief.

"Yep! Sure did and sure could have!" he admitted with a smile.

"Then, why didn't you? Why all the drama? What if the judge would not have allowed you to testify again in the evening meeting? Or what if there had not been an evening meeting?" I queried.

"Yes, it might have played out that way, I guess! But my boys were ready to carry them in any time I called for them---at the end of the afternoon session or at the beginning of the evening meeting. Even if the judge had refused, he and all the others would have been so curious as to the contents of those boxes, as they came in anyway, that they would have had to allow them to be presented as evidence!" he explained.

"Then back to my earlier question! Why did you wait until the evening session?" I asked again. "Why not the afternoon session?"

"To be honest I wanted the crowd to see what we have been through all these months. I wanted their emotions to take a roller coaster ride with us. I wanted them to go from thinking Clark Compton was undeniably guilty to then thinking he was lily-white in his innocence, and then to know beyond any shadow of a doubt that he was truly guilty, and what a scoundrel he was. I wanted them to experience a greater dislike for Clark Compton and what he had done to us, by first seeing what a con man he was, as his lawyer so easily conned them as well, even after they had heard the truth. I wanted them to see how they so easily rejected the truth in favor of the con man's lies.

"I am convinced that men come to see the reality of hypocrisy only by seeing the expert ability of the enemy to disguise himself as an angel of light. Once a person has been conned by the enemy, he will never be the same! As it has been said, 'Con me once and it's your fault, but con me twice and it's my fault.' Today's professing church is too gullible, as they will believe any Tom, Dick or Harry who comes along claiming to tell the truth. They will even more quickly side with the deceiver than with the one preaching the truth, without even stopping to analyze the evidence in comparison with Scripture. Maybe this will teach all those here today of the need of discernment as we live in this world of falsehood and hypocrisy all around us. I know what it is for I have lived with it for years in Comptonville. May others learn from this experience the same thing, and be delivered in the future from the deception and lies of the enemy!"

I dared not ask any further questions concerning the relationship between Mr. Compton and his mother. I was sure he loved his mother, and whatever the circumstances were of her encounter with Mr. Compton, it was enough for him and his father and the Lord to know the whys and the wherefores. I did ask him one more question.

"Is there any possibility that Clark Compton will fight this document you brought to court today?"

"Let him, if he wishes, but it's a hopeless case. The best law firm in the state handled the elder Mr. Compton's business, and there is no way that Mr. Compton's will can be broken. The words in the will and document and other legal papers are so clear, I don't think any lawyer could or would touch it."

As I sat down for a few moments almost totally exhausted, I looked at George and his depth of knowledge. I recalled God's providence in this whole journey. I even looked at Sam and his wife, still embracing, and recalled how he got saved in the middle of this mess, and then became a key figure in the providence of God to find and get the books to us just in time. I turned to Dink, and found him sitting down also.

I could only say to Dink, "Look what God did!!!!"

He answered in his usual manner saying, "Yeah, all by faith and prayer! Ain't our God good!"

Then he added, "Preacha, I gots one of dem sayins' fer you dat I been savin' fer just da right moment!"

Faith grows with us...
Put it to work by reverent and faithful praying,
and it will grow and become stronger and stronger
day by day.
Dare today to trust God
for something small and ordinary
and next week or next year
you may be able to trust Him
for answers bordering on the miraculous...
The man of small faith may be simply the one
who has not dared to exercise the little faith he has.
A. W. Tozer

56 Postscript!

It took some time for all the results to develop from the recommendations of the meeting just described. But when all was said and done, we again could only say, "Look what God has done!"

Obviously, the seminary board of trustees was not a law court, and therefore they could not deal with all the legal matters of the situation. The seminary presidents did, however, rewrite their premature resolution, this time listing the numerous charges against Clark Compton. This in turn led the Mid-City Baptist Seminary trustees to agree with such charges and the demand that Clark Compton resign as president immediately, which he was forced to do. There were a few of his die hard buddies on the board, who refused to believe the evidence against him, but they were outvoted and smothered in their objections by the rest of the honorable and honest board members. And, further, a number of legal charges were brought against him, and not one charge against him was dismissed---all were brought before the courts to hold him accountable, and all held up in the court system.

George Carlson gave Mac his interest in Turnover News Agency, and then Mac bought out Clark Compton's interest in TNA as old Clark was scrambling to keep his financial boat afloat in the days, which followed. And Mac did write a series of articles exposing Clark Compton for what he was---a plagiarizer, a criminal, and a fraud in every way.

Finally, Clark Compton went to jail for the rest of his life! It was not only from the evidence, which we provided, but as all his former goons came out of the woodwork to testify against him concerning his crimes, hoping maybe they could cut a deal for themselves. There was enough evidence to sink a battleship. Plea-bargaining proved to be a great aid in getting the big man behind the scenes, who had hidden behind others over the years, letting them do the dirty work of his crimes. But when push came to shove at showdown time, and all the rats fled his sinking ship, Mr. Big Guy (in this case Dr. Big Guy) was left standing by himself on his leaky and sinking vessel.

Dr. Madison, the Chairman of the Board of the seminary, where Clark Compton had been president, finally called me, giving me a good-old-boy, syrupy sweet apology from himself and the whole board of the school, supposedly. Perhaps he thought I might go after the school and the board legally in some manner for their failure in the whole situation, but I would never have done anything like that. He showed his hypocrisy though, when he dropped the condescending statement saying the next time they needed a theology professor, they certainly would remember me. I could have guessed it at the time, that I would never hear from him again, which proved to be true. To be honest I had no interest in teaching at his school, and I chalked it up to promises people make with no intention of ever keeping them. It just makes them feel good to be able to say it, and I guess they think it makes the other person feel good to hear such things. But such is only another form of hypocrisy!

George Carlson died some years later, but his remaining years were spent enjoying the mountains, which he loved so much, and he even ran for mayor of Comptonville and won. Amazingly, he showed some gift of administration, and Comptonville began to flourish once again, as people returned to the beauty of a rural mountain setting, once the people regained control of their beloved community.

William Sangster V wrote his doctoral dissertation on his great-great-grandfather's theology, a theology he gleaned from the reading of all the commentaries. He then wrote a popular version of his dissertation, adding the story of his great-great-grandfather's life and the events surrounding it, including the Compton family's evil deeds and domination of the city of Comptonville for all those years. He included in the book, also, all we went through to uncover the crimes, which had been hidden for so long. And he even returned to pastor the First Baptist Church of Comptonville, before he went on to teach at a seminary.

Obviously, under Pastor William Sangster V's leadership, the memory of his great-great-grandfather's years of ministry at First Baptist Church of Comptonville, were fully restored to their rightful place in the history of the church. Plus all his commentaries were printed by a leading publisher, and all the unsold copies of the plagiarizer's books were recalled and destroyed. What a blessing to see the whole set of the Sangster books in the foyer of the town library, as well as in the hallway where all the church's pastors' pictures hung---including the picture of William Sangster. How sweet it is when justice is done in both directions---punishment for the wrong doer and vindication for the vilified innocent one.

As for Dink, he remained the "Dink," but he laughed and said kiddingly that he was getting too old for such adventures. But then when I reminded him that we may never have studied those passages on faith together, if not for this recent trial, he softened a little with a smile. Then after a meditative pause he said, "Does ya tink we can wait a few weeks or months before we'se face annuder one of dese battles wid da enemy? I tink I'm a little weary jus' now of da smell a paint an I knows I'm tired of waitin' in dat corner!" Obviously, he was referring to our having been painted into a corner so many times during this past adventure.

He then added after another moment of pensive thought and with a smile, "But I guess I'd rather be in da Lord's will in dat painted-in corner dan outta His will wid no smell of da paint or da discomfort of dat corner. So's I guess, its corner, here we's come again---sooner or later!"

As for me, I must have slept for two days after this ordeal was over! I felt like I was getting old, when I found it so difficult to crawl out of bed, even after that much time in the sack. I also found myself wondering, as I rested just those last few moments in bed, before rising to face the world again, if my writings would ever be plagiarized? Would my ancestors ever have to go through what we had just endured in the reclamation of the Sangster books?

From my misty mind I concluded in answer to that idea, "Nah! Impossible. No one would believe all we have been through was real or possible!"

And with that I turned over in bed to enjoy the reality of the moment---sleep for a few more hours!

Books Mentioned in This Journey Book

Belcher, Richard P., *A Journey in God's Glory* (Columbia, SC: Richbarry Press, 2005).

----------. *A Journey in Inspiration* (Columbia, SC: Richbarry Press, 1998).

----------, *A Journey in Roman Catholicism* (Columbia, SC: Richbarry Press, 2004).

----------, *A Journey in Providence* (Columbia, SC Richbarry Press, 1999).

*Mackintosh, C. H., *The Mackintosh Treasury* (Edinburgh, Scotland: Loizeaux Brothers).

----------. *Genesis to Deuteronomy: Notes on the Pentateuch* (Neptune NJ: Loizeaux Brothers).

*A Brief Note Concerning C.H. Mackintosh (CHM)

Charles H. Mackintosh, one of the Brethren writers, was born in October of 1820 in Wicklow, Ireland. He was converted to Christ when he was 18 years old. Eventually, he began a periodical, *Things Old and New*, of which he was the editor and main writer for 22 years. He died on November 2, 1896 and is buried in the Cheltenham Cemetery in the section known as the Plymouth Brethren plot. He was a dispensationalist, which ideology evidences itself at times in his writings, but his rich and spiritual insights concerning Biblical subjects and passages are well worth the reading, even by a non-dispensationalist.